THE KISTE AND OGAN SOCIAL CHANGE
SERIES IN ANTHROPOLOGY

Editors

ROBERT C. KISTE   EUGENE OGAN

University of Minnesota

Pertti J. Pelto received his undergraduate degree from Washington State University and his Ph.D. from the University of California, Berkeley, in 1960. His specializations are in research methods, psychological anthropology, technology, and social change.

Dr. Pelto held previous appointments at the University of Minnesota and Cornell University before moving to his present position as professor of anthropology at the University of Connecticut. His interest in ecology and conservation is of long standing and has resulted in his active participation in several environmental associations. In addition, he consults for the Community Mental Health Program of the Illinois State Psychiatric Institute.

His previous publications, both book and journal, comprise a list too lengthy to cite here and include *The Study of Anthropology* (1965) and *Anthropological Research: The Structure of Inquiry*, a book on methodology, first published in 1970 and currently in wide use.

THE SNOWMOBILE REVOLUTION

 Cummings Publishing Company

Technology and Social Change in the Arctic

PERTTI J. PELTO

University of Connecticut

Menlo Park, California

To the people of Sevettijärvi,
Herdsmen on Snowmobiles

Copyright © 1973 by Cummings Publishing Company, Inc.
Philippines Copyright 1973

Printed in the United States of America.
Published simultaneously in Canada.
Library of Congress Catalog Card Number 72-89138
ISBN 0-846-53755-9
ABCDEFGHIJ-AL-7876543

Cummings Publishing Company, Inc.
2727 Sand Hill Road
Menlo Park, California 94025

Foreword

Dr. Pertti J. Pelto's study is one of the initial volumes in the series of ethnographic case studies on social and cultural change published by Cummings Publishing Company. With the exception of a few small populations in the most remote regions of the earth, no society today remains unaffected by other social groups and the stream of current events. The studies comprising the series reflect this basic state of man's condition in the latter part of the twentieth century, and they focus on a common theme: the ways in which members of contemporary societies respond to and develop strategies to cope with modifications of their social and physical environments.

Each study in the series is based on field research conducted by the author. In addition to focusing his study around the theme of the series, each author is encouraged to develop other relevant theoretical implications of his material. Studies from the major geographical and cultural areas of the world are represented in forthcoming volumes, and the series provides a fairly even balance between literate and nonliterate societies. It is hoped that the studies will provide the materials from which some generalizations and conclusions about the processes of social and cultural change may be generated.

The present study is concerned with the small population of Skolt Lapps of northeastern Finland. The Skolts have had a long history of contact with members of large-scale societies. From the fifteenth century until World War I, the Skolts fell within Russia's sphere of influence. Subsequent shifts in political boundaries placed them in Finnish territory and then back again within the borders of the Soviet Union. At the outset of World War II, the Skolts cast their lot with Finland, and they were evacuated from Russia to their present location. The Skolts' responses to outside influences and the necessity of adapting to a new homeland caused some alterations in their traditional culture and life-style. Prior to the 1960s, however, and as Dr. Pelto observed during his first fieldwork in Finland, certain basic features of Skolt society had remained relatively stable. Their economy was based on reindeer herding. Reindeer were important for both subsistence and transportation in the harsh arctic climate, and males took great pride in their skills as herdsmen. Skolt society was also very egalitarian. As most individuals had equal access to crucial economic resources, there was little opportunity for the development of social or economic differences among them.

Beginning in the early 1960s snowmobiles were introduced into northeastern Finland, and the Skolts eagerly accepted the machines. On more than one occasion, Dr. Pelto has returned to the Skolts to observe the results. As his study reveals, this technological innovation has had repercussions on almost every facet of Skolt life. Their economic system, mode of transportation, and patterns of social interaction have been radically altered within a decade, and the egalitarian character of their society appears to be in the process of a major transformation.

Dr. Pelto's study focuses on the impact of the snowmobile on Skolt society, but he goes beyond the particular details of his materials and advances two generalizations about the processes of change which occur in situations wherein societies abandon locally available sources of energy for those which must be acquired from the outside. Further, and in contrast to most anthropological studies, Dr. Pelto offers his own evaluation of the effect of the snowmobile on Skolt society. He suggests that the consequences have been disastrous, and he outlines certain courses of action which could perhaps alleviate the situation. His suggestions are timely given the present concern with the impact of man's technology upon his environment, and they have implications which extend beyond the present study.

University of Minnesota
Minneapolis, Minnesota
June, 1972

ROBERT C. KISTE
EUGENE OGAN
Series Editors

Preface

I decided to write this book because I became convinced that a single technological device—the snowmobile—was bringing about a social and economic transformation of major proportions among the reindeer-herding people of Lapland. My attention in this research has been concentrated mainly in northeastern Finnish Lapland, on the Skolt Lapps of Sevettijärvi. These people used to depend on a livelihood from their small but well-watched reindeer herds, augmented by the abundant fish in local lakes and streams. However, changes in life-style have taken place since I first visited the community (in the middle of the 1950s) and they have been much more extensive than anyone would have predicted, yet they are merely a prelude to the still more striking changes anticipated in the future. Many different technological items, consumer goods, political developments, and other creations of the rapidly changing European cultural scene are having major effects on Lappish lifeways. And although it cannot be claimed that one particular mechanical contraption has been the single most important factor for change; nevertheless, the snowmobile in Lapland, and in other parts of the arctic, is outstanding in its speed of acceptance and range of impact.

Because the advent of the snowmobile is so new and so stark, we have the opportunity to examine the complex of related technological, economic, and environmental elements that brought about the transition to modern, cash-oriented lifeways. Instead of merely wondering what happened, we are close enough in terms of time to be able to study and to understand how the change actually occurred. Since all this has taken place in the past seven or eight years, what happened is so clearly etched in the increasingly anxious minds of the Skolt Lapps of Sevettijärvi that we can read the printout of the statistical changes *and* recapture something of the play-by-play course of events that has brought these people to the present stage of unremitting sociocultural change.

The argument that I wish to present in this book rests on the assumption that, whatever their origins, technological changes that shift production processes (in this case reindeer herding) from local, autonomous sources of energy to a dependence on outside sources, (for example, gasoline) will almost certainly have wide-ranging consequences on the social and cultural patterns of the affected people: the replacement of reindeer sleds by snowmobiles in Lapland is not just another technical replacement. It represents a substitution that is more powerful by several magnitudes than, for example, the adoption of gas lamps in place of kerosene or radios and TV sets in place of the former relative isolation from outside communication. The penetrating influence of snowmobiles has resulted in a process I will call "de-localization" of energy sources.

In the context of reindeer herding there is another significant element: the machines by their nature force the herdsmen into quite new and unprecedented relationships with the animals with which they interact to make their living. It is not just the people who have changed their ways of life; the reindeer also have reacted sharply to the presence of machines. This double impact compounds the sociocultural force of the snowmobile revolution.

To understand the many-sided influence of the snowmobiles we have to take a quite eclectic ecological approach to this instance of human social adaptation. The web of interactions among the Lapps, their new machines, and the reindeer takes particular shapes because of the physical landscape on which they operate. The social environment, made up of neighboring groups, structures of government and economic enterprise, as well as international boundaries, must be carefully considered in the picture. The structure of local social action, and the personal qualities of the individual reindeer herdsmen also contribute elements to a total ecological framework.

Although the central "cause" in this particular instance of sociocultural change has been the snowmobile, it seems to me that many other technological devices, especially those involving relatively large energy requirements, are likely to have effects similar to these when they impinge on previously more autonomous societies. These general outcomes, which I suggest are likely to occur among many peoples and places around the world can be stated as follows:

1. When modern factory-produced technological devices, especially those that are motor driven, replace man-powered and animal-powered machines in local production systems, the inevitable and very far-reaching consequence is a *de-localization* of essential energy sources. This creates greatly increased dependencies on the mac-

rocosm of commercial enterprise and political influence outside the local community.

2. As de-localization and technological development proceed, a likely concomitant is an increasing technical and economic differentiation among the individuals and family units seeking to adapt to these changes in their environment. Increased social stratification is likely to be a further consequence of these processes.

In order to document the transformations that I have labeled the "snowmobile revolution," I first provide some introductory remarks in Chapter One and then describe Skolt society prior to the advent of the snowmobile in Chapters Two, Three, and Four. The latter two are particularly important as they deal with the methods and technology of reindeer herding and arctic transportation before the snowmobile.

Chapter Five brings on the snowmobile and its spread throughout the Lapland arctic. Some of the characteristics of the innovators and the innovational circumstances are discussed. Snowmobile use and ownership must be considered within the context of the problems and techniques of upkeep and maintenance. Chapter Six is devoted to these materials.

All this is preliminary to the main focus of the book—the mechanization of reindeer herding. My assessment of the results, which I have come to see as a "reindeer disaster," is provided in Chapter Seven. The social, political, and economic effects of this disaster are then examined in Chapters Eight and Nine in statistical and qualitative terms, particularly as expressed in what seems to me a growing stratification of material wealth and economic resources in the community.

In an earlier day of anthropological inquiry I would have concluded my work with a general summary, Chapter Ten, couched in theoretical terms, hoping thus to communicate some ideas to the general audience of social science readers. But this time I must go a step further. As part of my debt to the Skolt Lapps I feel that I should take the ethically and pragmatically risky step of *recommending* some alternatives to the course of events now unfolding in that Lapland community. In making recommendations I am, of course, introducing a series of value judgments about "good" and "bad" in relation to aspects of life in northeastern Lapland. I am judging the "reindeer disaster" to be a "bad thing," and one which should be corrected. My recommendations are risky not only because of the value judgments involved. They also depend on my assessment of the pragmatics of reindeer herding. I have even presumed to make some judgments about different techniques of herding—which are hotly debated by Lapps who have years of experience in these matters. My suggestions about the possible future shape of reindeer herding, presented in the Epilogue, must of course be taken with great reserve (better to say suspicion) by persons who have practical interests in this part of the Lapland economy, but I feel that I can offer some opinions here because I have accumulated a fair amount of concrete data (both statistical and qualitative) from extensive firsthand contact with the activities about which I am recommending. No one is going to take my word for these things, but I set out some of these ideas nonetheless, in hopes that they might in some way contribute to the careful discussion of the future of reindeer-herding organization in northeastern Finnish Lapland. I very earnestly hope that the data and ideas that I set forth here might have some future positive effects for the Skolt Lapps.

In the many months that I have spent in the Sevettijärvi area of northeastern Lapland I have become indebted to a great many people for their information, their hospitality, and other help. At one time or another I have been offered coffee, food, or other hospitality by practically every household in the Sevettijärvi region, as well as in a number of houses in adjacent areas. I must now find some way to reciprocate the help given me by these people. The persons to whom I owe these debts are the protagonists in the dramatic events I describe in this book, and in part the intended fairness and effectiveness of my description is part of the bargain that I seek to strike with them.

One of those protagonists, whose limitless energies and innovative capacities have never failed to excite my admiration, found time among all his other activities, to try his hand at anthropological fieldwork. He has been an amazingly perceptive informant but has also derived some satisfaction from primary data-gathering work, including the administration of interviews and projective psychological tests. During the past twelve years, he has played a very large role in my fieldwork; his centrality to my research is quite congruent with his role in the events I want to describe. He was the first Skolt Lapp to buy a snowmobile and the first to buy an automobile; he was asked to be the chairman of the new reindeer association (he declined this honor). He is also one of the younger generation who participates in the embryonic Pan-Lappish activities enacted in annual summer meetings of the Nordic Lapp Council. Lest all these tendencies to "modernism" deceive anyone, I must mention that he was considered one of the most able herdsmen in the pre-snowmobile stage of the local reindeer economy.

Arto Sverloff, therefore, plays a front-stage part in many of the scenes that I recount in the following chapters. He is there because, like the ideal Lappish reindeer herdsman, he has managed to be "everywhere at once." Over time there has naturally developed some convergence between his interpretations and mine with respect to Sevettijärvi reindeer herding. In recent times I have developed the habit of checking my data and my interpretations with him to see if they seem reasonable to him. Nonetheless, I must hasten to protect him from readers who might blame him for whatever mistakes and biases appear in this work. The mistakes and biases are mine, not his. He must not be held responsible. I have cross-checked the data with many informants and many personal observations, as well as with available statistical materials. Any blame for weaknesses in my work must be born by me—not by the protagonists in the Sevettijärvi scene. Nonetheless the strong presence of Arto and several other actors in these episodes of life in Sevettijärvi is a strong reminder of my very great indebtedness to them all.

I have made several attempts to construct lists of the Lapps and Finns (and others) in northeastern Finland whom I especially wanted to mention and to thank in this public form. Each time, however, the list grows and grows until it becomes obvious that it is pointless to try to enumerate them all. However, I wish to express my sincere gratitude to all of those people. They are most directly responsible for whatever success I achieved in this research, and they are also the people who made my several sojourns in northeastern Lapland enjoyable and extremely rewarding in personal terms. I must be content in the hope that this book might in some small way be of benefit to everyone in the region, at least by reminding the urban people of Finland and elsewhere that the things they decide in their legislatures, and the products they send to Lapland, have powerful and often unforseen impacts on the peoples of the arctic backlands.

Several Finnish scholars, as well as researchers from other areas, have helped me with information, critical comments, and other forms of colleagueship. Among these I owe special thanks to my long-term friend and fellow "lapinkulkija" Martti Linkola, and to his family. Other Finnish colleagues and friends to whom I am deeply indebted include Pekka Sammallahti, Karl Nickul and his entire family, Asko Vilkuna and family, academician Kustaa Vilkuna and family, the late T. I. Itkonen, and Juhani Nuorgam and family. Other individuals who have aided me in this research and to whom I wish to express here my heartfelt thanks include Ludger and Linna Müller-Wille of the University of Münster, Tim Ingold of Cambridge University, and Michael C. Robbins of the University of Missouri. A number of researchers of the North American arctic have provided me with information about the impact of snowmobiles in their areas; these include Peter Usher, David Damas, Milton Freeman, Derek Smith, Lorne Smith, David Moyer, Richard Nelson, David Stevenson, Richard Hill, Lee Guemple, and Edwin S. Hall.

Financial support for my research trips to Lapland has come from a number of different sources. I gratefully acknowledge and give thanks to the following for their support: National Institute of Mental Health (Fellowship in 1960 and Small Grant Award in 1962); Wenner-Gren Foundation for Anthropological Research (travel grant in 1967); Graduate School of the University of Minnesota (small grant); the University of Connecticut Research Foundation (research grant in summer, 1971); and last but far from least, my parents, Jack and Jenny Pelto, for substantial loans during my first fieldwork in 1958–59.

The editor of this series, Robert Kiste, provided excellent, detailed, critical reading of the manuscript for which I am very grateful; and I also owe many thanks to Frances Hayward, who typed most of the original manuscript. Most of all I am grateful to my wife, Gretel, for the many many hours she spent in editing, re-editing, and helping me to conceptualize this book at every step of the writing process.

Mansfield Center, Connecticut   PERTTI J. PELTO

Contents

Illustrations

PHOTOGRAPHS

MAPS

CHAPTER ONE

_____

Introduction

Every environmental "niche" on the face of the globe poses special problems of adaptation for its human inhabitants. In all parts of the world people must devise ways to obtain food. In some areas predatory animals, insects, and other disturbing or dangerous creatures require technological countermeasures if humans are to maintain adequate states of health and security. In all areas, too, there are problems of getting from one place to another. The peoples of Oceania—in Micronesia, Polynesia, and other far-flung islands of the South Pacific—developed a high level of ocean-going competence with sailing canoes. Many river peoples in the Amazon and other inland water systems achieved great technological effectiveness in water transportation.

In the dry areas of North Africa, the Near East, and Central Asia various cultural groups developed a number of different means of land transportation, particularly through a high level of technical effectiveness with domesticated beasts of burden. Camel riders and horsemen have been able to travel rapidly across great areas of steppe and desert, bringing warfare, new religions, and other cultural influences. Downs (1961) has documented the importance of animal-riding technology in the growth of complex warfare in the Eurasian continent.

New inventions in ocean travel leading to more seaworthy ships and improved navigational equipment were important in bringing about the great periods of migration and new discovery, notably in the spread of Mediterranean peoples beyond the Straits of Gibraltar to the Azores and to the British Isles in the time of the Phoenecians, and again in that great explosion of exploration and travel—the Age of Discovery. Within a strikingly short period of time Portuguese, Spanish, French, British, and other sailors were sailing the islands of the South Seas, discovering the New World, and bringing trade routes between Europe and the Far East into existence.

The very recent history of modernization also includes some striking technological changes in transportation. Within the memory of many people living today, the automobile was established as a means of land transportation replacing horse and carriage. The burgeoning popularity of "horseless carriages" in the early part of the century brought new demands for paved roads, an increasing degree of population mobility, and a wide range of beneficial and not-so-beneficial side effects. It is hardly necessary to document the extensive social changes and the new environmental problems that have developed as a result of the automobile. In this same period the airplane greatly influenced both peaceful and warlike human activities. Rocket travel into outer space and human landings on the moon are the most impressive manifestations of this latest phase of technological development.

Many other kinds of inventions in transportation have had wide-ranging effects on human cultures. Frequently the most apparent effects are brought about by the simple fact of speed; when men suddenly find themselves able to travel three or four times as fast as formerly, there are bound to be important repercussions in the structuring of social action and behavior. A second major effect arises from the increased ability to carry heavy loads of merchandise, personal belongings, and weapons. Before the internal combustion engine and related technologies transformed human transportation systems, people were generally very limited in what they could carry with them. Now the average "modern man" can move very widely *and* maintain an awesome inventory of personal goods. The list of clothing, supplies, and equipment carried by the typical

American vacationing family would surely arouse the wonder
of Central Asian nomadic tribesmen.

Transportation in the Arctic

Until very recently inhabitants of arctic areas depended
for the most part on centuries-old, nonmotorized means of
transportation. Throughout the North American arctic, dogsleds have been a principal means of winter travel and hauling.
In subarctic areas toboggans and snowshoes were standard
travel equipment, particularly among the Indian populations
of inland Alaska and Canada. In northern Eurasia, on the other
hand, reindeer sleds and skis have been the primary equipment
of winter mobility.

In Eurasian arctic areas domesticated reindeer have probably been used for pulling sleds for many centuries. They were
also used as pack animals. In certain areas of Siberia, among
Tungusic-speaking peoples, a larger-sized variety of reindeer
has even been used as a mount in hunting and traveling. Ar-
chaeological evidence shows that skis were in use in northern
Europe at least two to three thousand years ago, although they
may be much older.

Modern gasoline-driven vehicles, including aircraft, have
been plying their routes in the Far North for several decades,
but their services have been much too costly for the ordinary
arctic traveler, and their operations are severely restricted by
weather conditions and other factors. Automobiles, trucks, and
busses of course require costly roads. Because of the high costs
of operation and maintenance, neither aircraft nor ground vehicles could replace the versatile and inexpensive traditional
means of transportation. That was the situation until the beginning of the 1960s.

The idea of vehicles that can "go anywhere" or that can
get off the road and travel through field and forest has occurred
to nearly everyone—especially to those of us who have found
ourselves hopelessly stuck in one of the rush-hour traffic jams
that have become commonplace in our way of life. We've often

dreamed of turning off the road and going through fields, avoiding the bottlenecks inherent in even the most modern road systems. Military vehicles capable of traveling through all kinds of terrain have been known for a long time, since in the exigencies of war no costs are spared, and damage to fields, fences, and other man-made features are discounted. Tanks, half-tracks, and rugged four-wheel drive "Jeeps" provide examples that have not been lost on those dreamers who have wished for the day of personal all-terrain vehicles. Modern military transport equipment has also been designed for travel through bogs, sand dunes, jungles, and other difficult environments. Military all-terrain vehicles have, therefore, provided some of the prototypes that engineers have followed in trying to develop machines for travel in ice and snow.

The Invention of Snow Vehicles

Carl Eliason of Wisconsin patented one of the first successful "snow toboggans" in 1927 (Encyclopedia Canadiana). Eliason's toboggans were brought into the Far North in small numbers, particularly during the 1950s; but they were unreliable and had little impact on arctic transportation systems. The major design feature which delayed the development of one-man snow vehicles was the problem of finding a really effective, lightweight, and inexpensive engine.

Another inventor who worked on motorized snow vehicles was the French Canadian, Joseph-Armand Bombardier of Quebec, who had been experimenting with snow vehicle designs since the 1930s. One winter Bombardier's small child became ill and had to be rushed to the hospital. Travel through the snow drifts was an agonizingly slow process with horse and sled. The child died on the way to the hospital. Bombardier was determined to develop a machine that could travel rapidly under even the most adverse winter conditions. By the 1950s he was successfully manufacturing a seven-passenger "snow bus" (selling for $7,500) that operated on half-tracks and had a front turning mechanism consisting of metal skis. These vehicles were too expensive for private use, but they were used in government mail routes and passenger transportation in both the Canadian and northern European arctic areas during the 1950s and the early 1960s.

In 1958 Bombardier found an extremely efficient two-stroke, single-cylinder engine manufactured in Austria that seemed ideal for a small snow vehicle. This engine made possible the development of the "Ski-Doo," the first successful one-man snow vehicle, which was put into production around 1960. This machine held a near monopoly in the first years of the "snowmobile revolution," so the name "Ski-Doo" became the usual generic label for one-man snowmobiles among many arctic peoples in both Europe and North America. Many other large and small manufacturers quickly entered the field of snowmobile production, and by 1965 a large variety of different types of vehicles were in arctic and subarctic use. It is estimated that by 1970 there were a million snowmobiles in use in North America.

Although inventors such as Bombardier and Eliason were concerned with practical matters of winter transportation, the first dramatic spread of snowmobiles came about largely in winter recreation. In the northern tier of states—Minnesota, Wisconsin, Michigan, Vermont, New Hampshire, Maine—and in the adjacent provinces of Canada, a variety of new winter activities developed to take advantage of the new transportation device. Touring in the snowy backlands, cross-country racing, travel to ice-fishing locations, and other recreational activities utilizing snowmobiles have brought a large increase in winter activity to some rural regions.

While many rural dwellers were quick to appreciate the economic possibilities of snowmobile-related tourism in the north, serious problems arose in its wake. The new access to backland areas has brought about noise pollution, destruction of private property, damage to plant and animal environments, and many other ecological side effects. In most areas a rash of legislation has been enacted to control the problems created by this new technological device. In some places severe restrictions have been placed on the use of snowmobiles as hunting vehicles. The Finnish legislature, for example, totally bans carrying weapons on snowmobiles.

The Snowmobile in the Far North

Arctic people, including most Eskimos, Indians, and Lapps, cannot usually afford to spend hundreds of dollars simply for recreation. Since most snow vehicles cost at least $700 when delivered to arctic areas, they would have had little impact if they had been limited to recreational activities. However, in a number of arctic areas these vehicles were put into use for a wide range of transportational needs. Government agents, teachers, medical personnel, forest rangers, and other people whose work required extensive travel found that snowmobiles are easier to manage and provide much more rapid transporation than dogsleds or reindeer.

Observing these uses of snow vehicles, the native peoples of the Far North began to experiment with the machines for their own purposes. In northern Canada and Alaska some Eskimos had had extensive contacts with machinery in connection with military or other governmental activities such as DEW-line construction, road building, and the maintenance of military bases. Some of these people had, in the course of these experiences, earned enough cash so that they could afford to experiment with snowmobiles in hunting and trapping activities. In northern Europe Lappish reindeer herders, too, observed the examples of the first snowmobiles that came into their area in the beginning of the 1960s and perceived the possibility that the vehicle could be used directly in reindeer-herding operations.

The adoption of snow vehicles has been extremely rapid, nearly completely displacing the entire complex of dogsleds and reindeer sleds that seemed irreplaceable until 1960. Not everyone in the arctic has converted completely to snow vehicles, of course. In some areas the people cannot afford the high cost of purchase and maintenance; in others, the terrain is too rugged and difficult for snowmobiles. In any case the style and

extensiveness of snowmobile use varies widely with differences in environmental conditions throughout the arctic.

In those areas where the snowmobile has come into general use, it appears certain that there will be widespread social
and cultural effects. The factor of high cost alone has very
great significance. It seems clear that one immediate effect of
the "snowmobile revolution" has been to create a sharp rise in
the need for cash in Eskimo, Indian, and Lappish communities.
This increased dependence on cash, in turn, is likely to have
far-reaching effects on other features of socioeconomic organization. (Of course, the need for cash did not originate with
the introduction of the snowmobile; but the cash demands of
motorized winter transportation are very great, compared with
the modes it replaced.) We may also expect many changes in
social interaction patterns and other aspects of behavior because of the striking difference in mobility of snowmobiles as
compared with animal-powered sleds.

In this study I will examine the impact of snowmobiles in
an area of northeastern Finnish Lapland in order to describe in
detail some of the most important ramifications of this technological innovation. I do not claim that the effects of the snowmobile can be entirely isolated from the many other social,
cultural, and economic changes going on in Lapland. General
modernization is affecting many other aspects of lifeways in
these areas. However, the impact of the snowmobile is itself so
striking and has enough visible, material concomitants that
some generalizations can be made and some hypotheses tested.
By focusing on a particular small region of northeastern Lapland it is possible to look at some of the differences in snowmobile use that are associated with different kinds of ecological
settings. I would hope that this case study can serve, then, as
a source for further hypotheses and suggestions for research in
other parts of the arctic.

In making this study of snowmobiles and their socioeconomic consequences I am motivated in part by a concern over
the neglect of technological data in anthropological research of
the past several decades. Even though the massive influence of
technological development on all aspects of our lives is abun-
dantly clear to everyone—layman and social scientist alike—

anthropologists have made very few systematic investigations of technology. As Harris (1968) has pointed out, there is a strong nonmaterialistic current in anthropological studies of social organization, of cognitive definitions and taxonomic systems, of changes in world view and "ethos," and many other common research topics.

Most recently, however, the rising interest in ecological studies has drawn some of our theoretical attention to the study of environmental factors and other material conditions of human behavior. The work of Bennett (1969), Geertz (1963), Rappaport (1968), and Vayda (1969), for example, illustrates a promising shift from what I regard as an overbalanced concentration on social, ideological, and cognitive factors affecting human lifeways.

Most of the growing library of ecological studies quite rightly focuses on modes of food-getting in particular environments, with attention to the special requirements and characteristics of plants and animals that influence the cultural patterns of social groups. Geertz, for example, has examined in detail the technical aspects of wet-rice production in Java:

> ... the output of most terraces can be almost indefinitely increased by more careful, fine-comb cultivation techniques; it seems almost always possible somehow to squeeze just a little more out of even a mediocre *sawah* by working just a little bit harder. Seeds can be sown in nurseries and then transplanted instead of broadcast; they can even be pregerminated in the house. Yield can be increased by planting sheets and exactly spaced rows, more frequent and complete weeding, periodic draining of the terrace during the growing season for purposes of aeration, more thorough ploughing, raking and leveling of the muddy soil before planting, placing selected organic debris on the plot, and so on; harvesting techniques can be similarly perfected. ... (Geertz 1963: 35)

Ecological research on hunting-and-gathering, slash-and-burn agriculture, nomadic pastoralism, and other types of subsistence systems are of prime importance for understanding the forms of human cultural adaptations. However, I feel that transportation equipment constitutes a second major body of material technology that needs much more research effort from anthropologists and other behavioral scientists. The effects of transportation systems are particularly important now, in an age when fossil-fuel burning motors are being adapted for use in all parts of the world. We may be sure that the mechanization of travel will have very important *unintended* effects on peoples' lives, in addition to the desired increases in efficient mobility.

My frame of reference for this study, then, is a general ecological orientation, within which I treat human cultural behavior as a heterogeneous and flexible system of adaptive responses. Bennett (1969) has described this research orientation very clearly:

> A second meaning of the term ecology emphasizes adaptation or *adaptive behavior.* Here we refer to coping mechanisms or ways of dealing with people and resources in order to attain goals and solve problems. Our emphasis here is not on relationships between institutions, groups or aggregates of data, but on patterns of behavior: problem-solving, decision-making, consuming or not consuming, inventing, innovating, migrating, staying (*Ibid.,* 11).

> Out of these considerations flows another: how does one define or measure adaptation? Adaptive behavior can, as we have already implied, be defined in terms of goal satisfaction: if coping is successful, the people realize their objectives. In a market agrarian society, these objectives can be defined in terms of quantity of production; income; and consumption wants or needs. However, this is only one dimension of adaptation. A second, and equally important one, is the conservation of resources (*Ibid.,* 13).

Thus, in this study of snowmobiles, I will be concerned with examining the adaptive responses of different individuals to the new technical and economic situation brought about by the machines. It may be assumed, I think, that some people have adapted more successfully than others (and that such "success" can be identified); but, as Bennett noted, the adaptive successes of a population with regard to new machinery must also be weighed against the future consequences.

As suggested in the Preface, one main hypothesis that I set out to examine in my study of the "snowmobile revolution" can be stated as follows: That an intrusion of a significant new technological system, particularly one that depends on outside fuel sources for its maintenance and operation, will tend to generate *inequalities* in individual techno-economic capabilities with a resulting shift toward social stratification.

Many of the elements of modernization experienced by the Lapps in recent years have contributed to an increasing social differentiation, but some of the early developments in the snowmobile revolution appeared to have especially powerful implications for the growth of socioeconomic inequalities.

The more general ecological question around which the study is organized can be phrased: Using snowmobiles, can the Lapps of northeastern Finland preserve their reindeer-herding system in an economically and socially efficient form without serious and maladaptive effects on their reindeer, themselves, and their environment?

CHAPTER TWO

Northeastern Finnish Lapland: The Skolt Lapps and Their Environment

The Skolt Lapp community of Sevettijärvi is located in the northeastern corner of Finland (see Map 1), bordered on the north by the Utsjoki reindeer people who live in the northernmost tip of Finland and on the northeast and east by a narrow corridor of Norwegian territory that separates the Finnish Lapps from the Soviet Union. The territory is part of Inari commune (county); the government seat is Ivalo, a market center about 140 kilometers southwest of Sevettijärvi. A second, smaller community, Inari, is the nearest town, located some 120 kilometers from Sevettijärvi on the arctic highway that cuts through Finnish Lapland and continues into northern Norway.

The area lies just north of Lake Inari and is bisected by the northern boundary of coniferous forest. The southern half of the Sevettijärvi region has a relatively thin pine and birch forest covering the rocky landscape; in the northern part the pine trees disappear almost completely, leaving the landscape to small birch, willow, and other stunted arctic growth. Innumerable lakes and streams give beauty to the landscape and provide abundant fishing waters as well as flat surfaces for travel routes. In general the lakes and waterways are oriented in a northeast-southwest direction, interspersed with low ridges, none higher than about 200 meters.

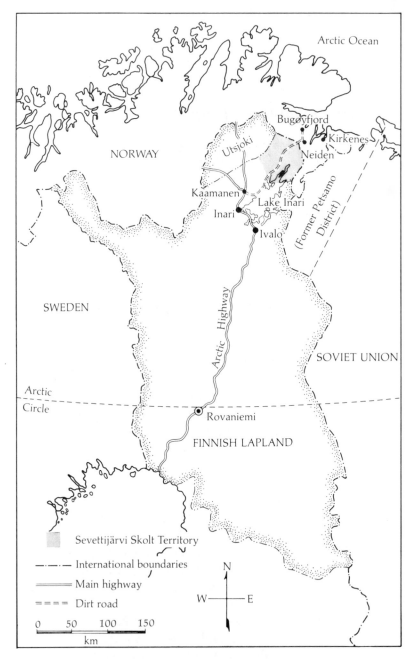

Map 1. Finnish Lapland.

Beneath the thin growth of coniferous and birch forest, the rocky ground is covered with a thick layer of various grasses, reeds, lichens, and other small growth. Numerous peat bogs are interspersed among the hundreds of lakes, so that boots are practically essential for walking in the backlands during summer months. These bogs are the most favored habitat for cloudberries (Rubus chaemaemorus), an extremely flavorful and valuable wild "crop." Market prices are often as high as $2.50 to $3.00 per liter. Other berries, especially blueberries and red whortleberries, are important mainly for household consumption.

Temperatures in this area range from a maximum of about +80°F during the warmest days of summer to an occasional –35° to –40°F in the coldest part of the winter. Frequently winter temperatures are between +15° and –5°F. The Arctic Ocean is not far away, and its open waters moderate the climate somewhat making this one of the warmer areas of Lapland. The average July temperature in the Sevettijärvi region is about +55°F, and the average February temperature is around +10°F (Platt 1955:334). Since the entire region lies some 200 miles north of the Arctic Circle (69° to 70°), there are about two months of continuous sunlight in the middle of summer and a corresponding period of sunless days during wintertime. Even the darkest days of winter have a few hours of gray daylight however.

Frosty nights sometimes occur in the middle of summer and become more and more a threat to berries and other delicate vegetation in late August and early September. Ice does not begin to form on the lakes until October, and the first snows may not come until November in some years. By December, however, the ground is usually covered with several inches of snow, and the ice on the lakes has already served for nearly a month as a natural highway. The average depth of snow cover is about sixty centimeters, and the average duration of snow cover is 210 days. The full breakup of snow and ice usually comes early in June, although travel conditions can become quite difficult during warm days of late May. The spring breakup results in periods of up to two or three weeks of restricted travel conditions, during which both winter and summer routes are nearly impassable.

The People of Sevettijärvi

Most of the people in the Sevettijärvi region are Skolt Lapps (approximately 335 people in 1959). Their language is closely related to that of the Inari Lapps to the southwest. Although these two peoples can understand one another (with some difficulty), their speech is mutually unintelligible with the Tundra Lappish language of the people living farther north. Nowadays the people of Sevettijärvi are nearly all bilingual, although there are a few old women who speak very little Finnish.

The Skolt Lapps generally resemble other Lappish populations in their physical appearance. They are, on the average, shorter than Finns and other northern European populations. Males average about sixty-two inches; females only fifty-seven inches (Lewin, Nickul, and Eriksson 1970). They have darker hair and darker eyes than Finns, although light-colored eyes predominate. Compared to Asiatic peoples, the Lapps are light eyed and light skinned.

The Skolts are relative newcomers to the Sevettijärvi region. For centuries they lived in an area known to them as Suenjel, which lies east of Lake Inari in territory that had been under Russian control from at least the fifteenth century until World War I. When Finland won her independence in 1920, this area, the Petsamo District, was included as Finland's corridor to the Arctic Ocean; and the Skolts suddenly found themselves to be Finnish citizens. The residue of the centuries-old Russian influence remains in their family names (Gauriloff, Sverloff, Osipoff, etc.), their Russian Orthodox religious practices, and their preference, at least until recently, for tea over coffee. Some of the older men served in the Czar's army and can speak a few words of Russian.

The Skolts fought in the Finnish army against the Russians during World War II and were evacuated from their Petsamo homes in 1940, when the area became a war zone.

Photo 1. A Lapp reindeer herder pauses for a smoke during a roundup.

When the war ended, the peace settlement imposed on the Finns by the victorious Soviet Union included the return of the Petsamo corridor to the USSR. The Skolts were given an opportunity to return to their Sovietized Suenjel territory, but they chose to remain in Finland, even though this choice left them homeless. After temporary settlement in several more or less unsatisfactory locations, they were finally granted a permanent home in the sparsely inhabited backlands around Sevettijärvi.

The area was less rich in fish, game, and reindeer pasturage than their former territory, but it was felt that the local natural resources would support them provided that the Finnish government assisted them in rebuilding their homes and subsistence economy. A chief problem in restoring their economic viability involved developing new reindeer herds, since most of their animals had been lost in the war. In 1949, the fifty Skolt Lapp families who founded the new community moved into their new homes—neat, red-painted, two-room cabins—scattered along the seventy-odd kilometers of lakes that run from the north shore of Lake Inari to the Norwegian border. A school, health center, and a few years later a church were built near the center of this linear settlement. A privately operated store and the government post office added a bit of settlement nucleation. Ten families are located within a kilometer radius of the school, so this "village" has become the center of communications for the area.

Each family has its own plot of land (small crops of potatoes are possible if late August frosts do not nip them too badly), and each household is allowed to build fishing cabins at selected sites on the many backland lakes. The surrounding country is owned by the Finnish Forest Service, but the Skolts have free access to the forests for firewood. Logs for building storage buildings, fishing cabins, and other structures can be obtained free, although a permit must be requested for timber-cutting. For purposes of reindeer pasturage the area is open to all legally registered owners without charge.

In addition to a few families of Inari and Tundra Lapps, who are long-term residents of the region, there are eight or nine Finnish families whose homesteads date back to the turn of the century. More recently, the number of Finns has been augmented by three schoolteachers, a nurse, and three store-keepers.

Social Organization

Most of the approximately fifty Skolt households consist of nuclear families. In 1959 two or three families included married sons or daughters and their spouses and children. Each nuclear family claims ownership of its own reindeer, fishing equipment, and other subsistence materials. Brothers and other kin sometimes aid one another economically, but theoretically, each household is self-sufficient. Although several households have usually cooperated with one another in certain aspects of herding, this cooperation did not include joint ownership or any other form of economic communalism.

The Skolt Lapps recognize kinship groups that are faint reflections of patrilineages. For example, the Semenoffs are descended from a common ancestor through male lines, and members of this "lineage" are not supposed to marry within the patriline. Two different Sverloff lineages are recognized since the two cannot trace descent directly from a common ancestor. Aside from this mild expression of patrilineal organization, the Skolt Lapps tend to be quite bilateral and flexible in economic and social interaction.

Although the Skolts are recognized as having a special status in Finnish law, occupying a separate "territory" to which access by other persons (for homesteading, economic activity, etc.) is restricted, they have been fully vested citizens of Finland since 1920. They vote in national elections; they are drafted into the Finnish army and are eligible for all the rights, obligations, and welfare services enjoyed by other people in Finland. Thus, they receive free or inexpensive medical services, free schooling, family allowances, pensions, old age assistance, and other services. They are even dependent on the outside world for their church services; the Orthodox priest travels to Sevettijärvi for approximately four or five services per year, of which the Easter rites are the most important.

In the days before snowmobiles there were no automobile or cart roads connecting the Sevettijärvi area with either Norwegian or Finnish settlements. The snow bus that plied the area in winter for the Finnish postal department traveled across frozen lakes and bogs and then followed a crude roadbed within the Sevettijärvi territory, making the 100-kilometer trip from the arctic highway twice a week. The "roadway" used by the snow bus disappeared during spring breakup, resulting in a month or more of very difficult travel conditions before the lakes and streams were open for summer boat travel. In the summer, mail and passengers were carried by motor boat on Lake Inari and then along a string of smaller lakes in the Sevettijärvi area. Only four portages (a total of about six or eight kilometers) were needed to make the boat trip from Inari to the village. Air travel also was available, but at rather high cost in both summer and winter. Small, single-engine, private planes carried supplies and passengers, sometimes bringing in perishable merchandise such as eggs, fruits, and vegetables, which could not be carried by reindeer sled. People in need of emergency medical attention were also occasional passengers on these planes.

Travel by plane and snow bus was confined to the main route from Sevettijärvi to the market centers on the arctic highway. Travel in the backlands (and locally between houses) was accomplished mainly by reindeer sled and skis in those earlier days.

Making a Living

One of the most rapidly changing aspects of life in relatively non-industrialized parts of the world is in the sphere of economic relations. Whether we are concerned with Lapp reindeer herders, Mexican peasant farmers, or Indonesian fishermen, it is almost certain that large elements of the economic organization of 1960 are, by now, very much modified. Anthropological descriptions are thus likely to be out of date by the time field data are published. In order to provide a background for recent transformations, especially as related to the impact of the snowmobile, the following section outlines main aspects of Skolt life-style as it appeared in 1958–59, the period of my first fieldwork in the community.

In prewar days the Skolts depended heavily on fishing for a major part of their food supply. Fish was a mainstay of the diet throughout the summer, but extensive ice fishing during fall and winter also provided a significant part of nutrition. The lakes and streams of Suenjel were said to be exceedingly rich in whitefish, char, lake trout, and other species. In the Sevettijärvi region, however, the people discovered that the supply of fish could not support their population. The lakes closest to their homes became seriously depleted, and by 1958 even more distant lakes showed signs of declining productivity. Nonetheless, fish continued to be a very important part of the local diet.

The reindeer provided the second major source of food. The Skolt Lapps have always considered themselves to be reindeer herders above all, even though the total food intake of reindeer meat was probably less than that provided by fish. Reindeer herding and related activities occupied a major part of their time. The management of reindeer herds was also central to their definition of themselves as a distinct people.

The usefulness of reindeer was not limited to food. As already noted, draught and pack reindeer were a principal means of transportation until very recently; and reindeer hides were important for making shoes, leggings, fur coats, and other articles of clothing. Sinews were used for sewing, and a few antler and bone items were manufactured. Also, reindeer meat, in relatively large quantities, was sold to traders and meat buyers for the cash needed to buy modern necessities, including flour, sugar, tea, coffee, and other staple foods, as well as many nonfood commodities. Thus, the reindeer industry was important in a number of different aspects of their mixed subsistence-and-cash economy. As long as a man had reindeer herds he could always get some food for his family, and he could also sell animals to get needed cash.

While most of the winter activities of Skolt men were centered on reindeer herding and related activities, they often sought wage work during the summer months when the reindeer were left free to wander in the woods and tundra. Some men were hired by the Forest Service to cut firewood, clear away windfalls, and plant seedlings. Work on the roadbed in the Sevettijärvi region provided employment for a number of men in the summer of 1958, and during other summers there were possibilities for roadwork, although not always in the immediate area. Many of the Skolts spent some months in construction labor on the large hydroelectric power plants that were built in the Soviet Union with Finnish labor. Very few men traveled farther south for wage work in those days.

With the Skolt women, especially the younger ones, the pattern was quite different. Since World War II there has been a strong tendency for the girls to look for husbands outside the local area. Over the years a majority of the Skolt girls have emigrated, either through marriage or by finding domestic work or other unskilled employment in arctic towns. One of the main opportunities for out-marriage was at the local military guard station on the Norwegian border which provided a steady circulation of eligible Finnish bachelors.

The difference between Skolt men and women in patterns of out-migration has been striking. Until the beginning of the 1960s nearly all of the young men returned to their homes after their occasional forays into wage work beyond the borders of the local community. Before 1960 only three men had migrated any distance from the local territory; two of these men maintained regular employment and residence in Ivalo, and one unmarried man moved from job to job in the cities of southern Finland. The disproportionately female out-migration pattern resulted in a relatively large number of bachelors in the Sevettijärvi population.

Although the Skolt Lapps had already experienced a fair amount of wage labor and other cash income in prewar days, they became more and more involved in a money economy during the late 1950s and early 1960s. In addition to occasional, usually highly seasonal, sources of cash employment, most of the families also began to rely to an increasing extent on income from old age pensions, disability payments, family allowances (baby bonuses), and other "transfer payments" from the government.

During the 1958–59 period, and again in 1962 when I had firsthand contact with the community, a number of important changes and developments had occurred, although these did not appear to bring about a fundamental transformation of the reindeer-herding-fishing way of life. The first telephone line into the community was built in 1959; each summer work was continued on the crude roadbed that was eventually to link the area to the arctic highway. (In 1962 it was a rugged jeep trail extending from Partakko to Sevettijärvi village; by 1967 it had been extended to Kaamanen, opening up the territory to vehicles from the arctic highway; and in 1970 the dirt-and-gravel roadway was extended to Norway, allowing an exceedingly bumpy and uncomfortable "through traffic" to the fiords and treeless fells of the arctic coast.)

Even before the new communications systems of the 1960s the Skolts had had fairly extensive experience in the wider world, especially during World War II, and they were well aware of the fashions, the ways of behavior, and the problems of their fellow citizens of Finland. Young men had regularly gone to serve their hitch in the armed forces, and members of the community had occasionally gone visiting or touring to the south, even though the relatively small amount of cash that individuals could muster did not permit extensive contacts in the cities and other costly places.

By the beginning of the 1960s there was also greatly expanded contact with tourists. Winter tourists came from nearby communities in Norway, especially during the Easter season to see the traditional celebrating of this isolated Lappish community. They also came to see the reindeer races, and occasionally some of these visitors went to reindeer roundups. In the summertime tourists, including hikers from Germany, France, and other countries, came into the area, sometimes hiring Lapps as guides and helpers.

By 1960, then, the Sevettijärvi Skolts thought of themselves as having come a very long way from the old days and traditional ways of prewar Suenjel. They spoke of cultural patterns and behavior in terms of "old model" and "new model"; and in the new model the distinctive headdress of unmarried girls had long since been discarded, people no longer remembered very much about the old games and dances, and some of the younger men professed to have little interest in reindeer herding. The wartime shock of losing practically all of their reindeer, their traditional territory, and most of their possessions had somewhat worn off, and there was no thought and no possibility of a return to that well-remembered, nearly autonomous life they had enjoyed in Suenjel.

The Egalitarian Nature of Skolt Lapp Society

The internal social system of the Skolt Lapps up to 1960 was basically that of an egalitarian society. By "egalitarian society" I mean that kind of social system in which access to the scarce resources of the region is, in principle, open on an equal basis to all those persons who have the physical and mental capabilities for exploiting them.[1] An important aspect of an egalitarian society thus defined is that "starting capital" is relatively unimportant as a factor influencing adaptive success and failures.

Hunting-and-gathering (and fishing) societies generally are egalitarian in this sense, since the main prerequisites for successful adaptation consist of personal skills, which are in principle available to everyone in the society. The equipment necessary for successful hunting and gathering is minimal; thus, everyone in the society has an effective chance to enter into competition for the available food supplies and other scarce goods.

Herding societies, such as the Lapps, are slightly less egalitarian than hunting societies since animals are required as "starting capital." However, many herding societies (and especially the Lapps) have mechanisms that insure nearly every able-bodied individual a chance to acquire "starting capital" of herd animals at an early age. For example, Skolt children received "first tooth reindeer," "name-day reindeer," as well as occasional gifts from godparents, other relatives, and other sources. Furthermore, newlyweds were usually given reindeer for wedding gifts, so that by the time an individual achieved

---

[1]Morton Fried (1967) and Marshall Sahlins (1958) use the term "egalitarian society" in much the same manner.

full adult status his acquisition of at least a small reindeer herd was assured.

Herdsmen need territory (pasturage) for their animals, but that, too, has been freely available among the Skolt Lapps throughout both prewar and postwar times. In Suenjel there were allotted territories for each family, and the old community had enough space for everyone. In the association herding system that has been in effect for the past twenty-five years, there are no "family territories," and an individual's reindeer can wander throughout the area at will. Land is thus a "free good."

Now, strictly speaking, the Lapps have, for a very long time, been living in a stratified society—as a relatively "lower class" within the larger socioeconomic system of northern Europe. But my argument here is focused on social differentiation *within the Lapp population itself.*

In most egalitarian societies there are a few relatively wealthy families, as well as a few poor families, in spite of their relatively equal access to resources. Among the prewar Skolts some people had a lot of reindeer and others had rather small herds. But these differences in wealth mainly reflected differences in the herding capabilities of individual householders rather than serious differences in basic access to resources.

In hunting-and-gathering societies, too, there are differences in wealth and prestige based on differential skills, wisdom, and other personal attributes; but these are not allowed to "get out of control," and the differences tend not to be inherited from generation to generation.

Among reindeer herders there are *some* tendencies for wealth and prestige to be inherited from one generation to the next, but the opportunities open to capable individuals have been great enough to prevent the development of wide differences between the rich and the poor. A further element in our definition of egalitarian society should be noted. As illustrated by the Lappish social and economic system, the wealthier, more prestigious individuals *did not control access* to the scarce resources in such a manner as to prevent poorer persons from bettering their status. Wealthier families had no mechanisms for exerting power or control over the poorer families. In a very real sense, individuals in the reindeer-herding-plus-fishing economy of the Skolt Lapps have struggled with the natural environment, rather than with their human neighbors, in seeking to better their lifeways.

The basic egalitarianness of Skolt Lapp social structure was particularly pronounced in 1949 when they were moved into the Sevettijärvi territory by the Finnish government. The people had lost everything in the war. Reindeer herds, except for a few accidental remnants, were gone; houses, equipment, and furnishings had all been left in the Soviet Union, and nobody had much in the way of cash. Furthermore, the houses provided by the Finnish government were uniform, emphatically egalitarian, two-room log cabins. As donations of fishing equipment and reindeer were received, they were distributed according to obvious need, based on family size. This again underscored the leveling of economic situation produced by the vagaries of war. (A small group of families had managed with great risk to save a few of their reindeer from the old territory, but it gave them only very slight economic advantage, if any, over the rest of the population.) To all appearances the distribution of the donations that got the Skolt Lapps started again were fairly and equitably carried out.

By 1958–59, ten years after the Skolts came to Sevettijärvi, some significant socioeconomic differences had emerged. The number of reindeer per household was quite varied, reflecting some very real differences in reindeer breeding "luck" during the early 1950s. Some of these differences may have included the possession of a few extra reindeer at the outset in 1949, but for the most part the families with the most reindeer quite clearly had able and active herdsmen, as was apparent in the various aspects of reindeer husbandry that I observed in detail from January 1958 to April of 1959.

By 1958–59 other differences had begun to emerge in addition to differences in numbers of reindeer. The once totally uniform houses had not changed with regard to number of rooms; but some of them had acquired paint, wallpaper, and other trimmings that made them appear "more modern" and well kept, in comparison with those homes in which only minimal home improvements had been attempted. The total inventory of equipment had become somewhat differentiated; a few families had acquired motors for their boats, and by 1959 the first motor-driven saws appeared in the area. The people who acquired these new technological devices appeared to be characterized by considerable "entrepreneurial spirit," for the men with motorboats often engaged in hauling for hire. These were also homes in which a considerable amount of new construction (outbuildings, boats, and fishing camps) was taking place. We can say that, from an ecological point of view, the especially active families of the period 1958–59 were exploiting much more than an average share of the available environmental niches. However, nothing in the technology or the economic system made it possible for these successful families to put serious limitations on the adaptive alternatives of their kinsmen and neighbors.

CHAPTER THREE

Reindeer Herding
before the Snowmobile

Until the mid-nineteenth century the Skolt Lapps could well have been classified as reindeer *hunters* rather than reindeer herders, although "tame reindeer" were kept for transportation purposes as well as for decoying wild reindeer. As the wild herds gradually disappeared, the grandfathers and great-grandfathers of the present Sevettijärvi people began to build up herds of domesticated reindeer. Since the only practical method of reindeer-keeping in the age of wild reindeer had involved intensive care of well-tamed animals (with the aid of fenced enclosures), the style of herding that developed in Suenjel was based on the same general pattern. Herds were kept by individual families who depended on close man-animal interactions (Nickul 1970).

It is of considerable importance to keep in mind for later discussion of herding methods that reindeer tend to become habituated to the territories and/or migration patterns that they experience during their first year of life. Thus, the Skolts' reindeer did not engage in extensive migrations because the animals' ancestors, from early times, were not migratory. This contrasts markedly with the far-ranging, migratory reindeer of the western Lapps (for example, in Sweden).

By the time the Skolt Lapps became Finnish citizens (1920), the days of reindeer hunting were a distant memory, and some of the families had built up herds numbering several hundred head. These herds could not be kept in fenced enclosures, and it would have been unnecessary anyway since there were no wild reindeer to lead the domesticated animals back to a life of unbounded freedom. The Suenjel reindeer herds tended to stay within the boundaries of individual family territories, but those animals that strayed into neighboring areas were caught and returned to their owners in a series of reindeer exchanges.

> Reindeer ownership is recorded by a system of marks cut into the animals' ears when they are calves. Nowadays each earmark is registered with the *Paliskuntain yhdistys* (Union of Reindeer Associations), but in earlier times there was no such registry. Since there were at most only a few dozen different earmarks in Suenjel, every herder knew everyone else's ownership mark. It is extremely difficult for an untrained observer to recognize these marks, but experienced herdsmen can identify them quickly, even on fast-moving reindeer several dozen yards away. The number of earmarks has proliferated recently, partly as a reflection of population increases and partly because it is now customary to register separate ownership marks for children. Within any given district then, there are several hundred earmarks, in addition to which there are all of the earmarks from neighboring associations. No herdsman can remember every one of the hundreds of earmarks of his district, although some exceptionally able individuals can identify as many as 200 to 300 such ownership marks without consulting the little black registry books that herdsmen often carry. Figure 1a opposite illustrates some of the more common symbols which, in combination, provide thousands of different permutations. The earmarks of three Fofanoff men from prewar Suenjel, in Figure 1b, illustrate the way in which these marks cluster in families even though each adult male has his own unique mark.

The move from Suenjel to Sevettijärvi deeply affected practically all aspects of Skolt life, including, of course, activities related to reindeer herding. Some of the basic elements of the annual reindeer cycle that I observed during 1958–59 still reflected techniques and technology that had developed in the prewar days of intensive herding. Other aspects, however,

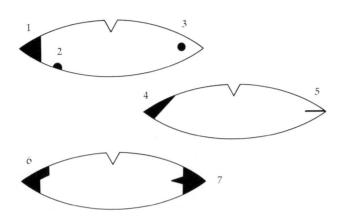

Figure 1a. Reindeer earmarks are recorded by stylized ovals, with left and right ears separated by the notch. Darkened areas represent the portions cut away or slit to create individual marks.

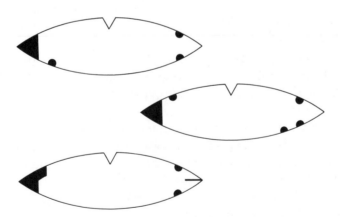

Figure 1b. Although each herder has a unique symbol, these three marks show the similarity of earmarks "owned" by three closely related men.

were extensively modified. Nonetheless, the magnitude of the changes required by the move to Sevettijärvi was considerably less than those of most recent years. In order to understand the dramatic changes brought about by the snowmobile, it is essential to begin with the pre-snowmobile practices. This chapter will be devoted to a description of reindeer-herding organization as matters stood until the early 1960s.

Patterns of reindeer herding are strongly affected by both the "natural" (physical and biological) environment *and* the social environment. Each has placed significant restraints upon and called forth adaptive responses from the people of Sevettijärvi as they worked to rebuild their herds after the war.

Terrain, Weather, and Seasons

The behavior of reindeer and, correspondingly, the organization of herding varies a good deal with the character of the landscape. For the men of northeastern Finland the basic contrast is between the open tundra and the pine-birch forest. As already mentioned, Sevettijärvi territory is bisected from the southwest to northeast by a string of lakes that has constituted the main "highway" through the region. This string of lakes is also the approximate dividing line between the forest and the open tundra.

In the tundra the winter winds sweep snow into hard-packed glaze that provides stretches of smooth travel surface for ski-men, reindeer sleds, and (in recent times) snowmobiles. The reindeer also find this terrain conducive to rapid travel, partly because lichens for grazing tend to be sparse and shelter from blizzards inadequate. The open tundra gives the herdsmen clear advantage over the reindeer in visibility and maneuverability. The birch and willow thickets, and the low hills and marshy valleys offer some hiding places for the arctic ptarmigan—which are snared and sent to gourmet tables in Stockholm, Helsinki, and Oslo—but the reindeer are easily located and maneuvered in these areas.

In contrast to the tundra landscape, portions of the forested hills and ridges between the "lake highway" and Lake Inari are very rocky, as well as rich in vegetation. Some places

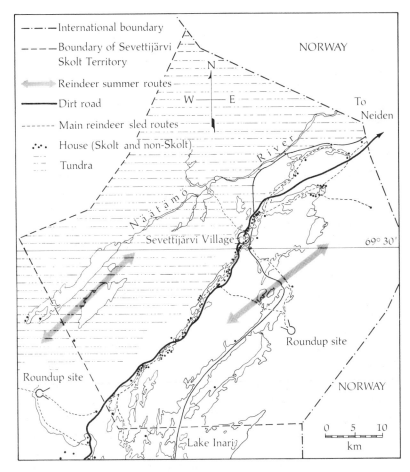

——·——International boundary
————Boundary of Sevettijärvi
        Skolt Territory
⇐⇐⇐Reindeer summer routes
————Dirt road
------ Main reindeer sled routes
∴·· House (Skolt and non-Skolt)
⁻⁻⁻ Tundra

NORWAY

To
Neiden

Näätämö River

Sevettijärvi Village

69° 30'

Roundup site

Roundup site

NORWAY

Lake Inari

0   5   10
km

Map 2.   Sevettijärvi Skolt Territory, Finland.

are best negotiated on foot until the deep snows of midwinter
have hardened sufficiently for sleds and skis. Herdsmen have
a difficult time picking trails in these areas, and the reindeer
easily evade their would-be captors. The balance sheet of visibility and maneuverability is on the side of the reindeer.

There are many other features of landscape that affect
reindeer herding. Peat bogs have little in the way of lichens for
winter grazing; high and windy open areas are relatively free

of mosquitoes in summer; lichens grow most luxuriantly in pine groves, especially on low hills; and so on. The innumerable Lapland lakes produce natural travel routes in some areas, natural barriers in others. In Map 2, for example, the narrow strips of land between larger bodies of water form "corridors" that constrain and direct the summer movements of the reindeer (shown by large arrows). Peninsulas, on the other hand, are sometimes used by reindeer herders as "traps" or "storage areas."

Changes in season and weather conditions markedly affect the behavior of both animals and men in Lapland. During the blizzards of early winter reindeer cluster together in larger and larger herds, and these aggregates move upwind in instinctive self-protection. As the snow cover deepens the reindeer find it increasingly difficult to dig through the snow to reach the lichens, their chief winter food. Once they've located a food supply, the animals are loath to move through deep snows to new grazing. Thus, the herds tend to stay in place and are more easily herded when snows are deep.

In the summertime the worst enemies of the reindeer are the swarms of mosquitoes and other insects. At the height of the insect season the animals gather in large herds to provide some measure of group protection. These herds sometimes mill around in wild and destructive confusion on especially warm and mosquito-plagued days. As the cooler days of autumn approach, the mosquitoes are killed by frost, and the reindeer disperse into smaller clusters until rutting time in October. During the mating season the females are gathered into harems (sometimes numbering a hundred or more) by the strongest and most active bulls. Smaller bulls wander on the peripheries of these harems, occasionally challenging the exclusiveness of the dominant males' sexual control of the females. Meanwhile, the castrated bulls have gathered into groups of their own. At different times of the year, then, the nature of the reindeer "social groups" and, to a certain extent, the locations in which they are likely to be found are different. Also, the quality of the reindeer meat varies during the year reaching a peak of desirability in early fall, so that this consideration, too, plays a role in the cycle of herding activities.

The Herding Association (Paliskunta) System of Finland

Overlaid on the face of the natural landscape of Finnish Lapland is a social landscape consisting of fifty-seven reindeer associations (see Map 3). These associations, which are patterned somewhat after the Finnish producers' cooperatives, came into being because of a legislative act of 1898, in terms of which all of the reindeer-herding areas of Finland were divided into districts of cooperating reindeer owners. The structure of the associations is quite simple. Every owner in a particular district *must* participate in the association by paying "head" taxes to the association and managing his animals in conformity with general association (and Finnish) regulations. Since it would be physically impossible for an individual owner to keep his animals totally separated from other animals of the district, the herdsmen's fortunes are inevitably interwoven with the policies and practices of the association.

Each association owns and operates several roundup enclosures (we will refer to them here as "corrals"), and the organization hires herders to carry out the major operations of gathering the herds for roundups. In pre-snowmobile days the association herdsmen were all of generally equivalent status receiving equal pay for their work, which involved traveling from area to area by reindeer sled spending several days at each location skiing through the backlands in pursuit of the animals. Arto Sverloff recalled that the first time he worked for the association (mid-1950s) the pay was eight Finnmarks (about $2.50) per day, plus one and one-half Finnmarks for one's dog if the herder had an active reindeer dog accompanying him.

Until 1969 the major part of the territory around Sevettijärvi was included within the Muddusjärvi association, the membership of which consisted primarily of Inari Lapps and Finnish reindeer herders living west of the newly formed Skolt Lapp area. However, the boundary line between two adjacent reindeer districts passes very near Sevettijärvi village (see Map 3), so twelve Skolt families in the northeast corner of the

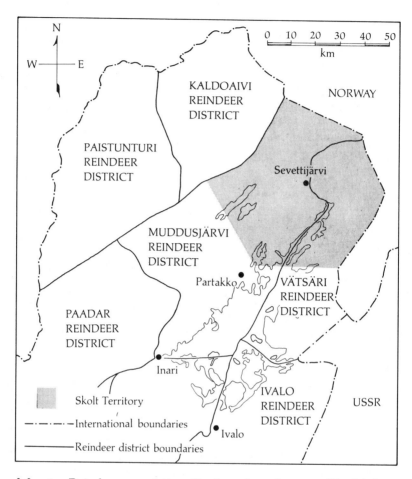

Map 3. Reindeer association districts of northeastern Finnish Lapland, 1968.

territory belong to the Vätsäri association, which also has a mixed Inari Lapp-Finnish membership.

Although the Skolts came to the Sevettijärvi area in 1949, they did not immediately become part of the Muddusjärvi reindeer herding. Since most of their herds had been lost in the evacuation from the Soviet Union, the Skolts were given donations of reindeer by the government and private individuals. These "gift reindeer" were obtained from various parts of Lapland, thus they would have returned to their home areas if they had been allowed to run loose. For a period of five years the Skolts maintained a fenced-in herd reminiscent of the old days when they still had to keep their animals separate from the roaming herds of wild reindeer. A fence was built across a peninsula jutting into Lake Inari, and the Skolt animals were tended within this enclosure. In time the herd came to number over 1000 head and had almost completely exhausted the winter pasturage within the fence. At that time (1955) the Skolt herds were turned loose into the Muddusjärvi district, since it was thought that they had become habituated to their new territory.

The joining of the Skolt herds with those of the rest of Muddusjärvi association brought about a very significant change in both herding and social relationships. Differences in ecological situation and general reindeer-herding techniques led to immediate conflict between the Skolts and their Lapp and Finn reindeer-keeping neighbors. The annual herding cycle that became stabilized during the following period (1955–60) included many features from prewar days, but it also reflected the increasingly pervasive effect of the association, a type of organization which had very minor reality for the Skolts in their previous family-herding autonomy.

The Annual Cycle: 1955–60

Since the reindeer were allowed to roam freely during the summer months, the season of reindeer activity began in the fall when herdsmen first went out to capture the relatively tame geldings which were indispensible as draught animals. Before there was much snow some of the geldings served as pack animals, but, for the most part, they were not used until several inches of snow cover permitted people to hitch up their sleds for travel, wood hauling, and the first fall trips to the trading posts. Early fall collecting activities were carried out by individual herders on their own initiative, although it was understood that autumn activities could not begin without the authorization of the association.

In November, as soon as travel conditions permitted, herders in the pay of the association (in groups of three to four men under the informal direction of a foreman) went out into the woods and tundra to begin gathering the herds. As larger and larger collections of reindeer were brought together, the animals were kept under constant surveillance for they are especially sensitive and likely to scatter during early winter when the light snow cover still permits rapid movement. The lore of herding is full of reindeer that were almost ready for the roundup, but scattered to the winds because of blizzards or predators. In 1958–59 there were still a few wolves in northeastern Lapland, and even today wolverines occasionally attack the herds. A brief visit by wolves or wolverines could quickly undo the results of several weeks' reindeer collecting.

In the Muddusjärvi district there was usually a "north herd" and a "south herd," each of which often numbered several thousand reindeer. When word was received that large herds had been collected, announcements were placed in the Lapland newspapers that a roundup would be held at one of the corrals. Usually the north herd was brought in first, while the south herd was held back in the grazing area until the roundup processing of the first herd had been completed.

Map 4 shows the location of the herds, their routes to the general roundup area, and the "staging area" in which the herds were held while portions were taken to the corral in 1958. Since the north herd numbered several thousand, only about one third of these animals were driven into the enclosure at any one time.

The final drive to the corral was carried out in much the same fashion as the drive from the pasture areas to the staging location. A bell-reindeer, led by a ski-man (or a herdsman riding in his reindeer sled) walked at the head of the herd, with the rest of the animals strung out in a long file behind. A large herd stretched out for a kilometer or more, with herdsmen riding and skiing (some with herd dogs) along the flanks to keep order. It was a slow-moving, majestic procession.

As the file of reindeer approached the opening to the "funnel fence," the lead herdsman quickened his pace in order to keep up the momentum as the suspicions of the animals

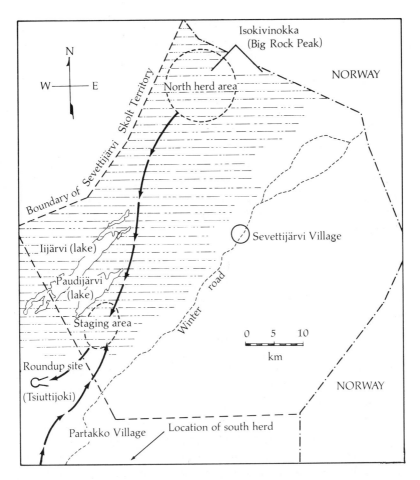

Map 4. Herd area, staging area, and roundup site, 1958–59.

mounted. At this point a sudden loud noise from the roundup camp or the appearance of a dog or other moving figure would cause the herd to bolt. When the end of the file cleared the mouth of the funnel fence, dozens of herdsmen hiding in the snow jumped up and ran into position at the entrance—closing the funnel with a human fence until the animals were secured in the secondary corral.

When the animals were finally lured into the roundup arena, the individual owners could begin to capture their own animals with lassos. The captured animals were pushed and dragged into small enclosures off the main corral area. There the owners slaughtered some for home use, sold several to meat buyers, and gathered the rest for tending in home herds. Calves tend to stay close to their mothers, so those that had not yet been earmarked could be identified (by their physical association with particular cows) and marked. There was considerable excitement in the first major roundups for the animals were still relatively fat and tasty, and they commanded good prices from the buyers. (Winter pasturage is always insufficient for reindeer so the animals lose ten to twenty percent of their weight by the time spring brings promise of new types of food.)

The roundups in pre-snowmobile days were "harvest festivals," in a sense, for the herdsmen were eager to find how many of their cows had as yet unmarked calves and how many reindeer turned up again after being "missing from roll call" the year before. Generally various negotiations and payments had to be made or collected. Since the roundups lasted anywhere from three days to two weeks or more, there was ample time to carry out the main business of locating and disposing of one's animals *and* to celebrate with friends and relatives not seen since the previous winter.

During the roundups the men lived in cabins near the corral, some of which served as public "coffee houses." Hot meals were sold by the proprietors of those coffee houses, although some herdsmen brought their own food supplies in order to cut down on living expenses. Liquor was usually available from part-time bootleggers, at least during the first days of the roundup.

Since there are always some reindeer that stray rather widely during the summer freedom, many of the Skolts' animals turned up at the roundups of neighboring associations. Sometimes there were also large numbers of "foreign" reindeer in the herds of Muddusjärvi men.

Food Sources of the Reindeer

Reindeer eating habits, like those of many other arctic animals, assume quite different patterns in summer as compared to the winter. Summer is, of course, the time of abundant food during which the animals graze on shoots, grass, young leaves, and many other kinds of green vegetation. The real feast that tops off the summer banquet is the mushroom crop, which in good years makes the reindeer fat and sleek in the fall.

After a brief flash of brilliant colors in autumn, the lush vegetation of summer fades away and is covered by the snow and ice of winter. Reindeer begin searching for lichens, their winter mainstay. Lichens grow as a mossy-looking yellow-grey carpet in most of the drier parts of the arctic. It is especially abundant in the pine forests and on the dry flatlands and low hills; it is much less prevalent in the peat bogs, marshes, and lakeshores. The reindeer dig through the deep snow with their sharp front hooves, after locating lichen patches with their keen sense of smell. Lichens grow very slowly; the recovery of an overgrazed area can take up to twenty years, and it is the weak link in the reindeer subsistence system. Thus, the limits imposed by the government on the various reindeer districts are based on the estimated carrying capacities of this one critical food source.

Reindeer with earmarks were generally returned to their owners or sold on their behalf, but the unmarked calves that strayed into neighboring territories were often "recognized" by the local herdsmen for their own, unless representatives of the owners were on hand to take vigorous countermeasures. In general the Skolt Lapps attended not only the roundups of the Muddusjärvi association, but also (in varying numbers) the corresponding activities in neighboring districts.

Table 1 lists the schedule of main roundups in the Sevettijärvi region for the 1958–59 season. The first roundup of the year was held at Petsikko corral. This was a new addition to the annual cycle, and it clearly reflected the growing tensions between the Skolt Lapps and the more westerly members of the association. The Skolts were strongly opposed to the Petsikko roundup for several reasons.

1. This premiere event of the herding season was intended especially for the sale of meat to Finnish meat buyers, who could drive their trucks directly to the site. The Sevettijärvi people, on the other hand, much preferred to sell their reindeer meat to Norwegian meat buyers with whom they had

Table 1.   Schedule of Principal Roundups in the
Sevettijärvi Region, 1958–59

Place	Association	Date
Petsikko (Muddusjärvi-Kaldoaivi border)	Muddusjärvi and Kaldoaivi (jointly)	December 2–21, 1958
Neiden (Norway)	Saalamo	December 4–15, 1958
Vätsäri	Vätsäri (Paatsjoki)	January 15–22, 1959
Tsiuttijoki	Muddusjärvi	January 27– February 9, 1959
Vätsäri	Vätsäri	February 19–23, 1959
Tsiuttijoki	Muddusjärvi	March 20–24, 1959
Some additional roundups attended by some Skolt Lapps that winter:		
Neiden (Norway)	Saalamo	January, 1959
Paistunturi	Paistunturi	February 10–12, 1959
Tshokkavaara	Kaldoaivi	January, 1959
Neiden (Norway)	Saalamo	February, 1959

long-established patron-client relationships that dated from old Suenjel times. This international trade took advantage of a Norwegian-Finnish agreement that allowed border residents from Finland to obtain duty-free, tax-free goods in their exchanges with the Norwegian traders. The precarious balance of the Skolt Lapp economy was very dependent on these favorable exchanges, which were not as important for the Westerners in the association because of their greater distance from the border.

2. Participation at the Petsikko roundup was especially costly because of the distance and the difficulty of bringing enough food to avoid paying the high prices for meals in the coffee houses.

3. The herd that was processed at Petsikko was turned loose instead of being transported back to the primary herding areas in the northeast. Thus, the Skolts were unable to bring home any animals from Petsikko for their own uses. Scattering

the animals also caused serious delay in the later roundups from which home herds were to be taken.

4. The animals that were turned loose in the Petsikko area would have to be gathered again and reprocessed in a later roundup, thereby enduring a second time the physical hardship of frightened running in the corral.

There is little wonder, then, that the Skolts felt the Petsikko roundup was extremely detrimental to their herding interests. The fact that they were powerless to stop this event dramatically underscored the significance of the reindeer association as a powerful new factor in their social environment.

At the completion of each major roundup (except Petsikko) small groups of individual owners jointly drove their animals to grazing locations within a few kilometers of their homes. By early February each owner had at least a portion of his herd near home, where they could be watched over in cooperation with kinsmen and neighbors. During the winter of 1959 there were eleven such "winter herding groups" in the Sevettijärvi area. The group of herders nearest the village center included about a dozen different households, but most of the groups consisted of three to five fairly closely related families.

The winter herds did not have to be tended continuously. The reindeer generally stayed together during most weather conditions, particularly in times of deep snow. Owners visited their herds periodically to carry out various tasks such as butchering, castrating bulls, and selecting geldings for training as draught animals. Often many days elapsed before the herd was visited again. These winter herds constituted the food storage and "cash reserve" system of the herders. Whenever supplies ran short, a few animals could be slaughtered for home use and for trading to the stores in Norway.

The final activity of the annual reindeer-herding cycle in the Sevettijärvi area was the spring calving. Since the individual owners had substantial control of their animals, it was usually possible to capture and tether the pregnant cows so that newborn calves could be tended, briefly protected from predators, and (most importantly) marked with the owner's

individual earmark. Calving time began in early May and
ended in the first week of June. Tending the cows—moving
them from one place to another for fresh grazing—is not difficult work, and the relaxation, gathering signs of spring, and
sight of newborn additions to the herd made this activity especially pleasurable. When the calf was a few days old and quite
spry, the cow and newborn could be turned loose for the summer. Calves that were very weak or sick at birth were tended
for a longer time until they, too, were ready for freedom.

By early June all of the animals had been loosed into the
forests and tundra, where they moved about freely until fall
herding began again. In some more southerly reindeer districts
spring calving operations were usually not carried out by
herdsmen; instead, the association herders gathered the animals in midsummer for calf marking. Such summer calf marking activities were not part of the annual cycle in Sevettijärvi
in pre-snowmobile days, although the practice was known to
the people because of contact with other areas.[1]

From the preceding description it should be clear that
there were two main phases to the reindeer-herding cycle (see
Table 2). The entire system depended on the work of the
association herdsmen who gathered the reindeer into large
herds as quickly as possible in the fall. These herds were kept
under surveillance for several weeks, even months, before they
were brought to the roundups. The roundups, among other
things, functioned to produce the official tally of owners' reindeer, in terms of which head taxes were paid to the association.
Once the roundup work was finished, the second phase of
herding began as the individual owners took control of their
animals and located them in winter herding areas near their
homes.

---

[1]The annual cycle of reindeer herding has been described in a number
of ethnographic monographs as well as in more poetic and artistic
works, such as Urpo Huhtanen's beautiful *Porovuosi* (Reindeer Year).
However, the annual cycle usually described in these works differs
substantially from the one I set forth here, mainly because of the
extensive, migratory, large-scale herding practices generally found in
western Lapland.

Table 2.   Main Events of Annual Herding Cycle, 1958–59

		Reindeer behavior	*Herdsmen's activities*
	June to September	Roam freely, widely, in summer grazing areas.	No herding (go to wage work, fishing, home maintenance).
Phase I	October	Rutting: bulls gather and defend "harems"; geldings wander in small groups.	Men set out to capture geldings for transportation.
	November to January	Gather into larger herds for winter protection.	Association herders collect the herds, watch over them, drive them to roundup enclosures.
Phase II	January to April	After roundup "processing" the small "home herds" are fairly stable and need little attention because of deep snows.	Owners bring animals to home herding areas, butcher, and transport meat to trading posts in Norway. Attend roundups to bring home more of their animals.
	May to early June	Calving	Herdsmen tether females, loose the rest of the herds, tend the mothers, mark newborn calves, then turn them loose with their mothers.

The intention of both association herdsmen *and* the individual owners was to sweep the tundras and forests *relatively* thoroughly in order to bring most of the animals into the control of the owners and to provide a fairly full accounting of reindeer. Long-standing "conservation practices" plus factors of terrain and weather insured that *some* "wild" reindeer always remained uncollected each winter, although by far the majority of animals could be found in individual winter herd groups by April, when the last of the roundups had been held.

Summary and Conclusions

For the Skolt Lapps of Sevettijärvi, reindeer herding up to the 1960s, can be divided into two main periods.

1. The prewar days in Suenjel, in which control and organization of reindeer-herding activity was largely in the hands of individual families.

2. The postwar period of rebuilding when they found their herding activities strongly affected by the Muddusjärvi association policies, in which they participated as a minority group with an ecological situation that frequently led them into conflict with the people in the western half of the association.

Although a careful consideration of the habits of reindeer makes it clear that many aspects of herding organization are closely tied to the habitual behavior and physical characteristics of the animals, there is still room for considerable leeway in animal management. In fact, the major changes in herding operations that mark the past fifty and more years of Skolt Lapp animal husbandry demonstrate the very great flexibility of the reindeer-herding ecosystem. Of course, *some* of the differences between Suenjel and Sevettijärvi herding practices have to do with differences in the physical environment, but the most important differences—especially in developments concerned with the Muddusjärvi association—have reflected aspects of the *social* environment. The greatly increased population (including a doubling of the Skolt population) as well as much increased articulation to neighboring groups and to the several levels of Finnish governmental structure have been major sources of modification in herding practices.

A key feature of the experiences leading up to the snowmobile age is the gradual deterioration of individual family control of the reindeer. While the loss of control to a certain extent freed men to engage in other tasks, another result of this trend has been the gradual depletion of herds because of inexplicable losses in calves plus the inability to carry out well-planned selective slaughtering and other aspects of growth-promoting husbandry.

It is fair to ask in this connection: How much can a herder diminish the *intensity* of his control over his reindeer and still keep up adequate levels of herd growth? Apparently the degree to which control of the animals passed into the hands of the association system during the 1950s was maladaptive from the point of view of the Skolts, for there were clear signs that their herds were not developing in anything like the way that herds had increased in prewar days. The association system freed men from many man-days of individual work, but the cost in herd productivity was severe.

In 1957–58 the Skolts in Muddusjärvi association had built up their total holdings to 2230 adult reindeer, plus a harvest that year of 700 calves. The figure in 1961–62 was 2167 tallied animals, plus 480 calves. This was not encouraging. Some of the men in those years expressed an increasing sense of futility, particularly in their attempts to cope with the complexities of association policy.

Throughout the 1950s and early 1960s the Skolts argued that they would be able to build up excellent herds again, if only they could have their own association separate from "those others" in the western end of the Muddusjärvi association. That hope for a separate association was not realized until 1969.

There is another aspect of the animal-land-human ecological relationships in Skolt reindeer herding that deserves mention. Much has been made of the migration patterns of the reindeer and of how they "force" the same migratory pattern on the Lapps in the mountainous areas of western Finland, Sweden, and northern Norway. We can ask, then, why have the Skolt reindeer (and those of most of the other associations in Finland) never migrated? The answer seems clear from what we know of the Skolt's history of reindeer breeding. *They did not let their small herds migrate* back in the days when these herds were small enough for intensive control. In fact, they could not afford to let their animals determine their settlement and movement rhythms since their annual semi-nomadic movements within the Suenjel territory were *attuned to the ecological demands of their fishing activities.* Once the breeding stock of reindeer had become habituated to a nonmigratory pattern, this ecological adaptation on the part of the reindeer was maintained through the social experience of each succeeding generation of animals.

The Skolts made this adaptation more "rewarding" for the animals by building shelters and smoky fires to protect them from mosquitoes during the worst of the summer insect period. The docility and territorial restrictedness of the reindeer was also maintained, and even intensified, through "selective assassination"—the more venturesome members of the herd were the ones regularly marked for elimination. This policy of "selective intensification of herd control" operated, in those earlier times, as a feedback spiral in which the increased control of the animals kept increasing the possibilities for further refinement of selective slaughtering. It was this feedback loop that the Skolts sought to institute in the new region, beginning on the peninsula beside Lake Inari. But the social forces impinging on them through the herding association prevented them from ever getting the system well started.

CHAPTER FOUR

The Challenge of Mobility

In the "old days" of Suenjel the Skolt Lapps had adapted to their physical environment with a semi-nomadic pattern of movements which took them from their nucleated winter village (December to April) to spring calving and fishing grounds; and then continued in a series of moves to other summer and fall locations within family territories. Each of the different locations within the family territory required a full inventory of equipment and supplies. From these several "home bases" the active herdsmen of the household traveled intensively through their territory, rounding up their reindeer in the fall. In those days there was no association carrying out roundup activities; each household relied mainly on its own resources in collecting its herds. When the people were all gathered in the winter village, the men had to make frequent trips out to their herds to keep away predators, to bring home fresh meat, and to carry out other herding tasks. They also made long market excursions to Norway.

Skolt Lapp life in Suenjel depended on a highly effective system of transportation. At least three different varieties of reindeer sleds were maintained, the most distinctive of which was the high-stanchioned *saan* that was usually pulled by three reindeer hitched abreast. This was the mode of travel for long distances on relatively open "roadway." For cruising in

Photo 2.   Draught reindeer were used with sleds to haul the large amounts of firewood necessary for a family. *(author)*

the hilly backlands in search of reindeer, the trim boat-shaped sled (Finnish: *pulkka*) was more effective. Freight was carried on the low-stanchioned, cumbersome freight sleds, much like the types now adapted for pulling behind snowmobiles.

The great emphasis on mobility as the key to successful adaptation was expressed in reindeer races and other contests, as well as in songs and folk tales that frequently told of both natural and magical travel. Many songs reflected the Skolt Lapps pride in their draught reindeer, sometimes with derisive characterization of their neighbors' supposedly inferior animals. The Skolts' recollections of life in Suenjel often dwell on the size, strength, and obedience of their draught animals in those bygone days.

The traditional courting and marriage rituals of the Lapps also symbolized the significance of mobility. To signal his intention to begin a serious courtship, a young man approached the girl's house by reindeer sled and drove around it three times, giving the girl and her family time to identify him and to quickly prepare for his visit. If the girl was interested and wished to open the way for further negotiation, she was supposed to go outside and unharness the draught animals for her suitor. At a later stage of courtship, the young couple exchanged draught reindeer, a gesture which indicated the couple was now seriously engaged. While other stages of courtship included gift exchange and other ritual activities, it is significant that two of the most important stages—the "beginning" and the formal engagement—were marked by ritual which involved the draught reindeer.

The concern with physical movement is also evident in many of the life histories of Skolts, some of which are constructed mainly of a series of journeys. Often the description of these travels dwells on difficult weather conditions, heroic efforts of powerful draught animals, and the occasional problems of effectively managing the reindeer-as-energy systems.

During my first fieldwork in Lapland, I was repeatedly impressed with the crucial importance of transportation of both supplies and people as a major adaptational challenge for the Lapland sociocultural system. Personal mobility, it was told to me again and again, is a main characteristic of the successful reindeer man: "You have to be able to get around." Winter ice and snow creates a very serious barrier to movement unless one has specially designed equipment. Even the reindeer have wide-spread hooves for extra footing in the deep snow, and other arctic-dwelling animals also have special characteristics that insure mobility (although some species find it easier to hibernate through a goodly portion of the winter).

Skolt Lapp song from Suenjel days in which Skolts boast of their draught geldings compared to those of the Inari men. (Itkonen 1948:565).

Inarin Porot

Inarin porot ne ovat
kuin kankeat heinäsäkit.
Kun lumi kynnen yli kohoaa,
niin miehet jo edelle hiihtämään,

mutta kas meidän ajokkaamme,
kenokaulat ja komeasarvet,
kun kinos yli polven ylettyy,
ne vasta laukaten menevät.

Inari Reindeer

Inari reindeer they are
Like stiff hay-bags
When over snow drifts they rise
The men already ahead are skiing,

But look at our draught geldings
Slim-necked and beautiful antlers
When the drifts over their knees reach
They really go runningly.

The change from Suenjel to Sevettijärvi included many new features in the transportation system. In the new location the Skolts found themselves much less isolated from the "outside world" than they had been in their old territory. Stores and market centers were considerably closer, and a number of gasoline-driven vehicles, including the bush plane and the postal department snow bus, maintained frequent contact with the Sevettijärvi community. Most of the Skolts stopped using their traditional *saan* sleds and relied instead on the simpler freight sleds, but this change was dictated in part by differences in the terrain of the new homeland.

In spite of these changes, the basic transportation system of the Skolts and the degree of emphasis on mobility remained unchanged. Skis and reindeer-powered sleds continued to be the transportational mainstays, and the rounds of herding activities, attendance at reindeer roundups, freight trips, and wood hauling still put a premium on the maintenance of effective draught reindeer and travel equipment. The need for transportational flexibility increased, particularly because of the increased importance of the reindeer-herding association with its meetings, roundups, and related activities.

Before the Finnish highway department completed the road from Kaamanen to Sevettijärvi, the main "roadways" were marked out along the lakes. The reindeer men drove along these sometimes elusive "highways" with their sleds, but more poorly equipped travelers, such as myself, had to depend on skis or pay the costs of transport on the Finnish postal service snow bus. As already noted, on special occasions air transport was used, particularly when sick or injured people needed to be rushed to the hospital in Norway or Ivalo.

Essential food supplies and other commercial goods followed the same routes by the same means. Reindeer sled trains carried nonfreezable supplies from the towns on the highway to the Sevettijärvi school and to the stores. Individual householders drove by reindeer sled to Norway to pick up supplies in exchange for their reindeer meat. Households that did not have able-bodied reindeer men (for example, widows without grown sons) had to hire relatives or neighbors to haul supplies for them. Supplies that would be damaged by freezing temperatures (fruit, eggs, potatoes, soda pop, milk, etc.) were carried on the snow bus in small quantities, but the more usual means of transportation for these items was air freight—a costly business. Hence these goods were rare and little used in pre-snowmobile days.

In addition to obtaining and transporting commercial goods each household also had to manage the transportation of naturally available supplies: water from the nearby lakes; fish and meat from sometimes distant lakes and herding areas; firewood from the pine and birch forests (usually no more than two to three kilometers from each house) and building supplies for fishing cabins and other facilities at the more isolated and inaccessible lakes. In spite of the fact that firewood is a "free good," hauling the birch and pine logs required a major economic effort.

The typical family of five to six persons required a minimum of twenty cubic meters of firewood per year, of which at least a third should be from dry, quick-burning pine. Firewood was extremely difficult to transport for any distance during the summer months so household fuel supplies were usually badly depleted by the time the first snows fell and sleds could again be used for hauling. Men began to get new supplies of firewood as soon as the first draught animals were available and a few centimeters of snow blanketed the ground. Through out the winter, when other work was not pressing, each householder continued hauling firewood, including stacks of fuel for fishing and herding camps. In later winter, before the spring breakup, it was essential to gather large supplies for the summer. Generally houses did not need to be heated during the summertime, but cooking still required a considerable fuel supply.

Freight Trips to Norway

The stores in the local Sevettijärvi area were important sources of food and other supplies, especially for the residents nearest the village center, but most families depended on the Norwegian trading posts for a large share of their staples. This provisioning usually required two or three major trips to Norway annually, the first of which generally took place as soon as reindeer had been slaughtered. Actually, the householders did not need to wait until they had reindeer meat to sell, for Gunnari's Bugoyfjord trading post would grant them credit in the early winter, confident that they would deliver meat when reindeer were obtained from the roundups. Trading relationships between Gunnari and some of the Skolt Lapp families dated from many decades earlier; they had made market trips of well over a hundred kilometers to reach Bugoyfjord from Suenjel.

The round trip from Sevettijärvi village to the Bugoyfjord trading post required about three days by reindeer sled (see Map 5). Each householder usually drove with at least four sleds —one for the driver and three to four sleds for freight. An extra draught reindeer, the "spare motor," followed in the rear of such a caravan. Concerning those pre-snowmobile freight trips, Feodor Petrov[1] of Sevettijärvi village recalled that he usually went alone, although men often got together for this expedition since the contacts at the trading post were likely to be expedited if several customers came in a group.

Hitching up his draught animals and preparing his equipment took several hours, so Feodor usually didn't get started for Norway until early afternoon. If the snow conditions were favorable there was no disadvantage to leaving late, since he

---

[1]All names of Skolt Lapps in this and following sections are pseudonyms except that of Arto Sverloff.

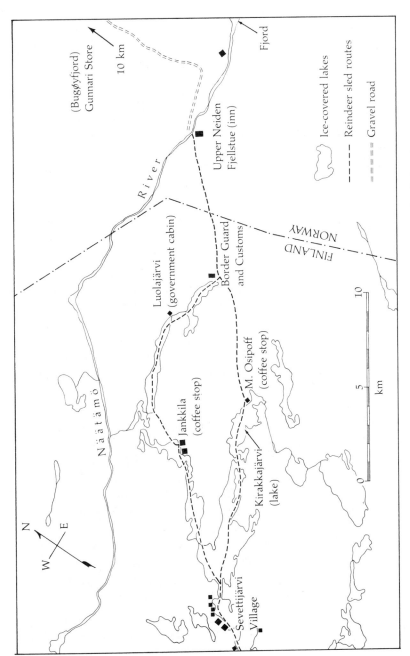

Map 5.   **Winter freight routes to Norway.** *Based on a sketch by Arto Sverloff.*

could easily reach his first night's destination in a few hours. Like most of the Skolt Lapps traveling to Norway, Feodor preferred to stop for the night at the travelers' cabin at the east of Luolajärvi (Cavern Lake), near the Norwegian border. There was good grazing for the reindeer, and the comfortable forest service cabin was available to all wayfarers without charge.

The next day Feodor drove the short distance across the border to Upper Neiden, at the road head. There, in the warmth of Sivertsen's lodging house *(fjellstue)*, he telephoned Gunnari's, from which a truck was dispatched to take him to the store, some twenty kilometers to the north. At this point several Skolt Lapps often went together for they knew that the truck would be sent more quickly if there were several customers.

While the men were at the store, their reindeer had to be tethered in places that were not particularly good grazing areas. The men nearly always carried small "loaves" of lichen, or perhaps hay or reeds, to feed the animals during the wait on the Norwegian side. They also used the food to catch the animals that were let loose, for the herdsmen preferred to tie only one or two geldings, allowing the others to roam about freely. The untethered animals usually came quickly when food was served.

After the chilling trip in the back of Gunnari's truck, the men were glad to spend several hours in the store shopping at their leisure and waiting as the storeman's helpers brought out the sacks of flour, sugar, and other heavy merchandise. Sometimes they were served coffee and sandwiches.

When all the customers from the Finnish side had been served, Gunnari's hired men loaded the freight into the truck and the men rode back to Upper Neiden. At that point a decision had to be made—either to drive directly to the Luolajärvi cabin or to stay the night at Sivertsen's *fjellstue.* If the hour had grown late, the men were satisfied to pay the 2 Kr. price (about thirty cents) for overnight lodgings. The *fjellstue* was one of their favorite social stopover places, and they often met Norwegian Lappish acquaintances and other interesting people there.

On the trip back to Sevettijärvi, Feodor estimated that he usually carried about 120 to 150 kilos per freight sled. His typical shopping list included the following (for a family of seven in 1959):

Flour—200-250 kilograms
Sugar—50 kilograms of cube; 50 kilograms of granulated
Tea—2.5 kilogram wooden cask
Coffee—5-10 kilograms
Kerosene (for lamps)—100 liter drum
Tobacco—2.5 kilogram case of pipe and cigarette tobacco
Margarine—30 kilograms
Butter—12 kilograms
Marmalade and jam—2-3 kilograms
Condensed milk—20 cans
Matches

Other items, depending on his mood and finances:

Crackers or cookies (for the children)
Frozen codfish (up to 10-20 kilograms)
Norwegian bread (several loaves)
Powdered milk (for the smaller children)
Sardines and sausages (for munching on the way home)
Scarves and cloth for his wife
Goat cheese (usually a 0.5 kilogram brick, a special treat for himself)

If weather conditions were favorable all the way, Feodor and his fellow freightsmen could drive back to Sevettijärvi by nightfall of the third day. On the other hand, the onset of a winter blizzard could slow down their travel so that the trip would end up taking five days. The men from Nitsjärvi, farthest to the southwest from the Norwegian end of the district, needed at least one extra day for the entire trip. There were other factors besides weather that might affect their time tables. Sometimes there was business to be taken care of in Kirkenes, requiring a bus ride to that busy arctic seaport. Also, liquor was more or less freely available on the Norwegian side, so there were men who preferred to spend a couple of extra days relaxing and celebrating before returning to the relatively alcohol-free backlands of Sevettijärvi.

Although most men followed this basic pattern of freight trips, there were many variations. Some drivers preferred to travel by way of Kirakkajärvi to visit friends on the way. Men

from the southernmost part of the territory sometimes stopped
for the night with relatives in Sevettijärvi; and they also made
several stops for coffee at houses of friends or relatives, particularly during midday when the animals had to be fed and
rested. Many of the Skolts liked to stop, at least for coffee, at
the houses of two Finnish families at Jankkila.

Every household (except those without able-bodied
herdsmen) generally took care of its own market trips to Norway. On the other hand, only the men with at least seven to
ten reliable geldings were likely to undertake freight hauling
for the local stores or the boarding school. These trips required
hauling hundreds of kilograms of supplies from Kaamanen, the
nearest point on the arctic highway. Occasionally, well-
equipped freight haulers arrived at Sevettijärvi with strings of
up to sixteen sleds after more than a week of steady travel.

Arto Sverloff recalled a bizarre and difficult freight trip he
made with Mitri Semenoff in which they fought a two-week
battle against the relentless advance of summer weather. They
had set out to get a shipment of baled hay and fertilizer during
the final days of winter in May. As they arrived at Kaamenen
to pick up the load, the weather suddenly turned warm. The
snows had already been melting, but as long as the nights
stayed cool they felt that they had a chance to make it back
to Sevettijärvi. But rain and warm weather continued day and
night; the "road" was rapidly turning to impassable slush.
Mitri and Arto decided to leave the road and risk their fortunes
with the waning days of lake ice on the broad reaches of Lake
Inari. If only they could get onto the ice (the shoreline ice was
particularly treacherous) they could proceed toward home on
a hard, flat surface. Soon they were lost. After several efforts
to locate a familiar shore at which to return to the safer, if more
difficult, traveling on land, they at last reached Partakko. There
they turned most of their reindeer loose and left some of their
cargo to be picked up during summer traveling conditions.
Dragging their few remaining reindeer with half-empty sleds
through the slushy quagmires, they finally arrived at Sevettijärvi almost two weeks after they set out from Kaamanen.

My field notes from 1958–59 are full of other descriptions
of routine hauling with reindeer sleds: Vasko Bogdanov was

hauling provisions to a summer fishing location; Nikolai Osipoff had built a fishing cabin in his backyard, to be hauled log by log to its permanent location when snows permitted; someone else was busy hauling posts for a new interdistrict reindeer fence; the Petroff men spent a day hauling lichen "loaves" to their yard from the backland location where they had stacked them the previous summer; and some of the Osipoff boys dragged a boat overland to the Näätämö River for summer fishing. Thus, in pre-snowmobile days a reindeer man's schedule of work included a very considerable number of days devoted to local hauling, in addition to his longer freight trips. Of course, many Lappish households contain more than one able-bodied male, and it should be noted that women sometimes participated in hauling activities also.

Travel and Communication

Freight-hauling trips usually gave people an opportunity to visit with other members of the community. Thus, news and information always traveled along with food and supplies. Often, individuals on skis or in reindeer sleds traveled from one location to another without much in the way of accompanying goods. Word of reindeer roundups and other important events had to be carried in person, particularly before the installation of the first telephone service in 1959. Sunday was a day for visiting, and families sometimes traveled a considerable distance to see friends and relatives. The children at the boarding school in the village center went home on holidays and occasionally on ordinary weekends. Some of the young boys at the school ski'd home at every opportunity, preferring the home environment for their weekend fishing and other recreation.

The reindeer-herding activities described earlier were, of course, the major activities requiring mobility. In addition to the main lines of herding effort sketched above, various kinds of subsidiary actions were carried on by herders as they crisscrossed the forests and tundra trying to catch sight of their own animals and those of kinsmen, hoping to identify unmarked

calves for later marking at the roundup, and locating the elusive small groups of reindeer that association herdsmen would
gather up and join to the larger herds.

Although reindeer herding was the emotional focus of
economic activity, most Lappish families of the Sevettijärvi
area relied at least as much upon fish as reindeer for their
subsistence. Portions of their fish supply were stored during
autumn, but ice fishing was important throughout the winter.
Since the best fishing sites were often far from the permanent
houses, expeditions to these locations frequently required a
day or two in traveling, in addition to the time spent fishing.

Wage work for the forest service, as well as other economic activities (including transporting tourists and other visitors) added to the long list of occasions that depend on the
arctic transportation system for success. Perhaps the full significance of this requirement does not come to our attention
until we experience for ourselves the helpless feeling and dependency of the outsider trying to move self and supplies from
one location to another without draught reindeer or other
equipment.

Two additional points should be made concerning the
travel and transportation system of pre-snowmobile days in
Lapland. First, it is notable that the basic means of travel for
ordinary individuals in arctic Lapland remained relatively unchanged from prehistoric times until 1960, in spite of the striking changes in the transportational means "out there" in the
industrial, urbanizing world. No significant improvements developed to replace sleds and skis, and even the fancy ski bind-
ings and boots seen in resort skiing areas were relatively
impractical (or actually dangerous) for Lapland reindeer herders.

The second point is that the isolation of Lappish populations, the sparseness of settlement, gives psychological as well
as practical impetus to individual mobility requirements. Although I have argued elsewhere that Skolt Lapps are psychologically adapted to traveling and working in solitude (Pelto
1964), they are not unsociable people; and the distances between settlements as well as geographical separation from the
events of the wider world have added to the psychological

salience of personal mobility as a means of maintaining inter-personal contacts. If we examine the mythology and folklore of Lappish peoples as compared with that of people in other parts of the world, it seems to me likely that the matter of travel and mobility will loom particularly clearly as a recurring theme.

Draught reindeer and skis provided an extremely effective transportation system for the Lapps. The maintenance of the system required great patience and skill, and only the best reindeer men had really reliable geldings that would "go any-where" and were easily coaxed into harness. Men with good strings of draught animals were accorded corresponding pres-tige, and their assured mobility was a significant factor in ac-counting for their herding success.

It is very important to note that the pre-snowmobile transportation system did not require importation of any fuel or other material from the outside world. Local energy sources (animal power) were harnessed by local means, and every herdsman was capable of building and maintaining his own sleds, harnesses, and other transportation equipment. The only drawback—and it was not seen as a problem in those earlier days—was that it often took a herdsman an hour or two to capture his "motor" for harnessing, and the hitching up and unhitching for grazing was a time-consuming task, especially after a long day of herding activity. On the other hand, Lapps did not have to hunt for food for their draught animals. This, in some respects, made the system more ecologically satisfying than the Eskimos' maintenance of hungry (and sometimes dangerous) dog teams.

CHAPTER FIVE

The Spread of Snowmobiles in Northeastern Lapland

During the fifteen months I spent in Lapland in 1958–59 there was no hint of the coming transportation revolution. Motorized transportation was already present in the community in the form of the postal department snow bus and the privately operated airplanes that served this part of eastern Lapland. By that time, too, some Skolt Lapp families were able to speed up their summer travel with the aid of outboard motors, but it was difficult to imagine that an economical motor-driven device capable of negotiating the difficult terrain of Lapland's winter would soon become available.

The first Bombardier Ski-Doo reached Finland from Canada in late 1961 or early 1962. The vehicle was on display to the interested public in Rovaniemi, the capital of Finnish Lapland. The purchaser of this first machine was a schoolteacher in the small settlement of Partakko, located approximately halfway between the arctic highway and Sevettijärvi.

News of the teacher's new machine spread widely in the weeks following its acquisition, for he apparently found it to be very practical. He had originally intended his snowmobile for recreational travel (especially for fishing trips), but it was soon clear that it could be useful for hauling wood from the forest and supplies from the store. The Partakko teacher was an excellent mechanic, and, as a bachelor, he probably had

more cash available for experimentation than many other people in the area. His mechanical abilities were documented by
the fact that his original machine was still in fine condition
when it was purchased from him by the Bombardier company
for their museum in 1971. By that time many other snowmobiles had been relegated to the newly created junk heaps of
Lapland.

The schoolteacher's experiences with the new vehicle
were not lost on other people in the area. The following winter
several persons purchased machines, including the nurse and
the forest ranger at Sevettijärvi, the postman in Partakko, and
four of the leading Lapp reindeer herders of Kaldoaivi. (Kaldoaivi is the northernmost reindeer district of Finland and is
composed mainly of Lapps from the Utsjoki area.)

The Kaldoaivi Lapps who bought machines were relatively wealthy reindeer herders, and all except one of them
were less than fifty years old. Since these prosperous herders
dominated the policies of their association, they had no difficulty in embarking on experiments with mechanized reindeer
herding. The wide-open terrain of their district is particularly
favorable for snowmobile use in reindeer herding, since there
are few places for the animals to hide from the swiftly moving
snowmobile herdsmen. This contrasts with the situation farther south (around Sevettijärvi) where the forested and rocky
terrain makes it much more difficult for herdsmen to locate and
control their animals by machine.

The structure of reindeer operations results in a great deal
of interdistrict contact among herders. The major roundups
always include official and unofficial delegations of herdsmen
from neighboring districts, and, in some cases, roundups are
held jointly by more than one association (as in the Muddus-
järvi-Kaldoaivi roundup at Petsikko; see Chapter Three). The
joint roundup at Petsikko in the winter of 1962–63 was probably the first one in Finland to be marked by the hum of Ski-
Doo motors.

In January 1963 the herdsmen of the Muddusjärvi association had great difficulty in bringing a large herd of reindeer
from the northeast end of the district to the corral at Tsiuttijoki. A herd had eluded the association men in the Isokivi-

nokka (Big Rock Peak) area about seventy kilometers northeast of the roundup corral (see maps 2 and 4). Normally it would take several days to bring a large herd from that location to the corral. This time, however, the Muddusjärvi association decided to hire one of the Kaldoaivi snowmobile herders along with two local machine owners, to bring in the reluctant reindeer from their refuge. The experiment was a success, and the herdsmen of the Muddusjärvi association were convinced that snowmobiles would be practical for reindeer-herding operations. The snowmobile revolution thus spread quickly from Kaldoaivi to Muddusjärvi.

In the winter of 1967, I received a letter from Arto Sverloff, one of the more active herders in Sevettijärvi. He wrote:

> This Sevetti has certainly changed since you were here. Reindeer work is thoroughly mechanized, no longer in the fall do we travel with pack reindeer . . . in the fall we do not rope geldings as we did when you were here before . . . Nowadays the reindeer work is done with the Ski-Doo, or motor sled; of these sleds there are many here now. The Sevettijärvi people have thirteen Ski-Doos.

The importance of this technological change for the reindeer herders of the area is evident from his following remarks:

> And reindeer work is done primarily with these motor sleds, but the results are fairly weak, compared with the earlier time when we used reindeer and dogs for herding. Now dogs are not used except on occasion . . . Nowadays we do not get our herds together in the winter except what little we get at the roundup, for they mix with the forest reindeer [unherded reindeer] and scatter into the forest . . . And we don't get our herds together and still the expenses are as before. Certainly earlier reindeer herding was completely otherwise. In those days we got our calves marked and our herds home. Now the calving comes to nothing since we don't get the cows tied. Not even any information about how many reindeer we have. No one wants to drive with reindeer anymore, but it must be by Ski-Doo or car. It is particularly sad since reindeer work is no longer reindeer work, but better some kind of play . . . If we don't get . . . changes in reindeer herding, we will be very poor reindeer men in a few years. This is the most frightening thing for us who live with reindeer herding.

Table 3. Number of Snowmobiles Acquired in the
Sevettijärvi Area, 1962–71[a]

Winter	Machines acquired
1962–63	2
1963–64	3
1964–65	5
1965–66	8
1966–67	16
1967–68	4
1968–69	9
1969–70	19
1970–71	6
	72

Total in operating condition as of spring, 1971:   70

[a]These figures reflect the *first acquisition* of a snowmobile by Lapp
and non-Lapp individuals in the area. Thus individuals' second
machines and trade-ins are not included. Many of the early machines
have been junked.

Because of the alarming note in Arto's letter, I was very
anxious to return to Lapland as quickly as possible. I immediately applied to the Werner Gren Foundation for Anthropological Research for a small grant that would permit me to spend
a few weeks in Lapland in order to find out more about the
snowmobile revolution.

On the day I arrived in Sevettijärvi in March 1967, people
were gathered for the traditional Easter reindeer races. This
turned out to be the last reindeer race in Sevettijärvi, for many
of the herdsmen has already gotten rid of their draught animals
and snowmobile racing had captured their interest. There were
about a dozen machines parked at the race scene, and the
occasional sharp sound of someone starting up his motor
caused the reindeer to be quite skittish.

In the course of my three-week stay in the area, I was able
to attend and participate in one roundup in which snowmobiles played a major role. During this period several men made

market trips to Norway, almost all of them by snowmobile. One day I photographed Jeffim Kiriloff driving to Norway by reindeer sled; it was the last time I ever saw this once familiar mode of travel.

During April, I was able to interview a large number of the reindeer herders in Sevettijärvi whom I had not seen for the past five years. I also arranged for fellow researchers from the University of Jyvaskylä to collaborate in gathering further information from all the districts in Finland. (cf., Pelto, Linkola, and Sammallahti 1968; Pelto and Müller-Wille 1972). A great many people expressed deep concern about the reindeer-herding situation, and it was clear that some of their herds had been seriously reduced. On the other hand, there was no consensus about the potential usefulness of the machines in direct herding operations. Some herders, especially younger men, insisted that with careful use the snowmobile would be an extremely effective and positive addition in all phases of reindeer work.

Table 3 presents data about the acquisition of snowmobiles in the Sevettijärvi area during the first years of the technological revolution.

The Spread of Snowmobiles in Reindeer Herding in Finland

The pattern of rapid adoption of the snowmobile in Sevettijärvi held true for much of the rest of northern Lapland as well. Figure 2 shows the rate of growth in snowmobile use in the northern herding districts. By the spring of 1968 there were about twenty-five reindeer districts (of the total of fifty-seven associations in Finland) in which snowmobiles were used in herding. We note on Map 1 that the capital of Finnish Lapland, Rovaniemi, is far from the scene of the first experimentation with snowmobiles directly in reindeer herding. The machines were introduced into herding operations by the Lapps and Finns of the northeast, (Kaldoaivi, Muddusjärvi, etc.) and diffused from there to the more settled areas to the south (Alaruikka 1964).

A frequent generalization concerning the introduction of new technology is that items tend to diffuse from population centers outward toward the peripheries. The reversal of this pattern in the case of the snowmobile seems to be the result of ecological factors and the relationship of herding to other economic activities. The districts in which the snowmobile was first put into use have a wide-open terrain where the machines have the maximum advantages of maneuverability; they are also the districts with the highest percentage of land devoted to reindeer herding as compared to other economic activities.

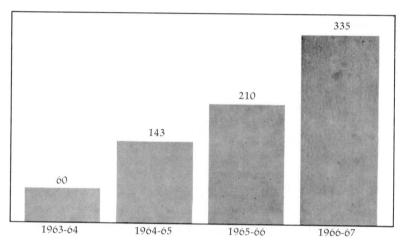

Figure 2. The number of snowmobiles in use in northern herding districts grew rapidly from 1963 to 1967.

These are the districts with the highest percentages of Lappish peoples in the population. (Kaldoaivi and the neighboring Paistunturi district have the largest percentages of Lappish population of any districts in Finland.) The districts farther to the south in Lapland are nearly completely Finnish in ethnic composition. Thus, the machine was adopted first in the area of "greatest commitment to reindeer herding" and spread from that "center" outward.

The Snowmobiles Replace Reindeer Sleds

The extensive transportation and mobility needs of Lappish reindeer men, as I outlined them in the preceding chapter, help us to understand the rapidity with which they seized upon snowmobiles as a complete replacement for reindeer sled transportation. (Eskimos in some areas of the Canadian arctic now operate with dogsleds *and* snowmobiles; Lapps practically never combine the use of machines with the maintenance of draught animals.)

The seeming advantages of the snowmobile are strikingly evident from the comparisons in Table 4.

Table 4.   A Comparison of Time Requirements for Snowmobiles and Reindeer Sled Travel

	Reindeer sled	*Snowmobile*
Preparation for a trip (including hitching up)	1–3 hours	5–20 minutes
Resting equipment on long trip	1–2 hours (rest and feeding)	15 minutes (refueling)
Evening maintenance during stopovers	1–1.5 hours (moving to fresh grazing)	none
Freight trip to Norway	3 days	5 hours
Sevettijärvi to Tsiuttijoki roundup site	1–1.5 days	2–3 hours
Kirakkajärvi to Sevettijärvi village	1–1.5 hours	20–30 minutes

The first snowmobiles, with their seven to seven and one-half horsepower motors, did not have large hauling capacities; nonetheless, the men found that they could haul at least 300 kilograms of freight home from Norway with these machines.

Later models are capable of pulling 600 kilograms of freight on open, fairly level roadway, such as the main travel route between Sevettijärvi and the Norwegian trading posts.

Quite early in the transition to snowmobiles the people of Sevettijärvi began to rely on the machines for a large part of the hauling that they had previously carried out with reindeer sled. Households that did not yet have machines hired snowmobile men to make their market trips for them. In 1964–67, when only a minority of households had machines, the technologically advantaged people had the opportunity to earn cash by hauling for their neighbors. Thus, the actual costs of purchase and maintenance of the snowmobiles were in part spread throughout the community. In fact, many of these first purchasers would probably not have been able to afford the payments and upkeep if they had not had opportunities to earn money from their neighbors and kinsmen through using the machines.

Traveling to roundups also provided income opportunities for the snowmobilers. The herdsmen without machines often preferred to pay for a fast ride to the roundup sites, rather than to hitch up their slow-moving draught reindeer. At the Tsiuttijoki roundup early in 1967 only four or five herdsmen arrived by reindeer sled even though most of the men coming from the Sevettijärvi end of the district did not own machines at that time. In these situations some diffuse factors, such as pride and prestige, played a part in peoples' decisions to stop using draught reindeer. On the other hand, many individuals felt that the speed and convenience of the machines was so clearly evident that they were economically justified in hiring transportation. As the revolution in transportation progressed, matters quickly reached the point at which choices between old-style and new-style transportation had become meaningless. With the exception of a few persons who expended very great effort to keep control of a few old and docile geldings, the Skolts had sold their sled reindeer to finance their new machines, so the draught animals were simply no longer avaliable.

By 1967 the use of sled reindeer was considered a curious anachronism in most areas of northwestern Finland. Among the Sevettijärvi people only four persons still traveled by reindeer sled that winter, and they said it made them feel conspicuous and uncomfortable. More serious was the feeling that they could no longer "keep up" in reindeer activities, since their slow pace left them almost completely out of the action.

In the Kaldoaivi district, "The last Lapp to ride a reindeer sled in Utsjoki was Heikki Aikio from Kultala, who—at the age of seventy—used it to 1966–67. But he also acquired a snowmobile in 1965–66, partly convinced by his young son twenty-five years old and partly by the economic and social pressure which was put on him by other Lapps in the reindeer district. He was at his age the most acknowledged reindeer herder in Kaldoaivi district. Although keeping up with riding in the reindeer sled, he also accompanied his son to reindeer round-ups on the snowmobile" (Müller-Wille 1970:6–5).

By the spring of 1971 all except twelve of the seventy households in the Sevettijärvi area (including the non-Skolt Lapp households) owned snowmobiles. Thirteen households maintained more than one machine. The veteran drivers had, by that time, graduated to their fourth or fifth vehicle, so that a brisk business in used machines was developing.

CHAPTER SIX

The Care and Maintenance
of Snowmobiles

The Skolt Lapps suspect, as do other observers, that the snowmobiles that arrived in Lapland in 1961 were engineered with an eye first to those weekend enthusiasts, the recreational users. Of course conditions of use in Lapland are different from the open, unchallenging terrain for which the machines were first designed. At any rate, the early years of experience with snowmobiles involved many repair and maintenance problems. One of the first Lapp snowmobilers in the northeastern region told of burning out *forty* V-belts on his first machine—apparently because of a misalignment of the motor mounts. In fact, nearly everyone among the earlier adopters paid out what would seem, from hindsight, to be an almost incredible outlay of cash to keep the machines going.

Arto Sverloff's first year of repairs (Table 5) is not atypical; he was able to keep his snowmobile operating even though frequent breakdowns often piled frustration onto frustration.

Two years later he traded in his first machine, after a season (1966–67) during which he had the expenses given in Table 6.

In spite of continuous maintenance problems, Arto kept his machine operating most of the time during those first years. He was able to use it enough of the time that his freight and passenger hauling contracts earned him a considerable profit.

Table 5.   Maintenance Costs of First Full Year of Snowmobile
Operation, 1964–65

Item	Number replaced	Unit cost (Finnmarks)	Total
V-belts	5	45	225
Drive track	1	450	450
Front spring	1	28	28
Bearings	1	10	10
Windshield	1	30	30
Drive chain	1	35	35
Steering shaft	2	9	18
Lamps	3	24	72
Total expenditures:			868
			($290)

Source: Arto Sverloff.

Some of the early adopters were not so successful as Arto in keeping their machines in running order; the other Skolt Lapp-owned machine in the community was out of commission most of the time during that first winter (1964–65)

Repair shops and spare parts were not available just around the corner in northeastern Lapland, particularly during the early 1960s. The dealers came all the way from Rovaniemi, 250 miles away, to sell their vehicles, and the machines sometimes had to be sent back to their shops for larger repairs. Spare parts came up the arctic highway by post bus, a two-day trip.

Fortunately for the Lapps, they had already had some experience with gasoline-driven motors before the arrival of snowmobiles. As noted earlier, a few outboard motors were in use by 1959; motorbikes and chain saws had also added to local machine maintenance experience. Outside observers have had reason to marvel occasionally at the technical abilities of the Lapps, just as North American ethnographers (and others) have frequently commented on the mechanical aptitude of Eskimos in similar circumstances.

Table 6.   Maintenance Costs of a Snowmobile, 1966–67

Item	Number replaced	Unit cost (Finnmarks)	Total
Replacement motor	1	670	670
Ski support	1	30	30
Rear axle	·1	40	40
Exhaust pipe; coupling	1	40 + 6	46
Drive wheels	2	60	120
Drive track	1	450	450
V-belts	5	45	225
Bearings	4	10	40
Accelerator wire	1	6	6
Lamps	4	8	32
Gasoline line	1	3	3
Windshield	1	30	30
Seat fabric	1	30	30
Total expenditures:	1	30	30
Total expenditures:			1692 ($423)

Source: Arto Sverloff.

From my limited experience with equipment breakdowns in Lapland, I can only sketchily illustrate some of the personal characteristics of Skolt Lapps that appear to contribute to their competent management of technical problems. Before I go into this account I must enter a disclaimer: not all Lapps are equally expert at machine maintenance and repair. Some individuals appear to be relatively incompetent in the handling of machines. On the other hand, there are those special people to whom friends, neighbors, and kin can turn frequently for technical advice and assistance.

A main characteristic that one finds among the more successful reindeer herdsmen is the quiet faith that every mechanical failure must have a cause, and that the cause will usually be readily apparent if one disassembles the machine. Furthermore, from earlier Lappish experience there has developed a curious optimism in the probability that naturally available materials—especially birchwood—can be used to repair almost anything.

My field notes and photographs from 1958–59 include, for example, the instance of the small bush plane that broke a propeller and damaged its landing gear during a mild blizzard at the Tsiuttijoki corral. The pilot and reindeer herders collaborated in whittling down the propeller to a more symmetrical shape; the landing gear was reshaped and tied with reindeer lassos. An optimistic holiday-spirited crowd of reindeer men watched confidently as the big bird soared away to "civilization" for more permanent repairs.

One drab afternoon of midwinter, while observing activities at the north herd (some twenty-five kilometers from the nearest settlement), I had the misfortune to break a ski. Given the sixty to ninety centimeters of snow, I was overcome with a feeling of helpless bewilderment. It seemed for a while that even the trip to our temporary camp, just a mile away, presented almost insurmountable problems.

In the evening the herdsmen quietly exchanged their views about the possibility of repair. It was agreed that my skis were badly worn and practically worthless in comparison with the kinds of equipment any thoughtful herdsman usually maintained. Nonetheless, I had to have skis, at least to get back out to the settlement. Somewhere, from somebody's backpack, a few nails were found. Next, the two halves of my broken ski were shaved down to provide maximum engagement of the two surfaces to be joined. This, of course, resulted in shortening the ski about a foot, but that was not seen as particularly detrimental. Then came the really crucial technological flash. An empty condensed milk can was opened at both ends and slipped over my ski like a sleeve. This metal "splint" was carefully pounded into place, particularly on the underside.

Once this feature had been adopted, the herdsmen felt that my ski would surely hold together. It did—and three months later, as I left the field to return to the United States, I was still using the same pair, although the tin can on my short ski tended to catch on icy ridges from time to time.

The tales that modern Lappish reindeer herders tell nowadays include a growing number of stories about "how I almost had to walk back when my snowmobile broke down." In a curiously large percentage of these cases, the herdsmen were able to put together some sort of makeshift repair that enabled them to drive home. Arto Sverloff recalls that one of his worst breakdowns in the backlands was caused by a broken rear axle. The axle was sheared off at a point very close to the bearing case. After carefully studying the problem, Arto decided that it might be possible to repair the break if he could find a short

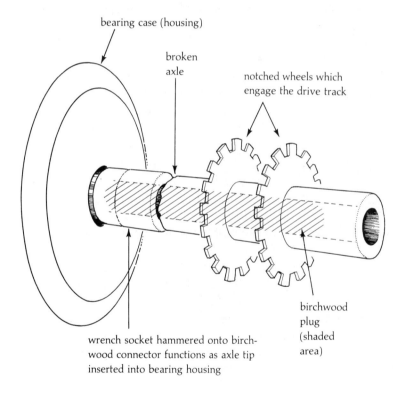

bearing case (housing)

broken
axle

notched wheels which
engage the drive track

birchwood
plug
(shaded
area)

wrench socket hammered onto birchwood connector functions as axle tip
inserted into bearing housing

Figure 3.   Temporary repair of a broken axle, using a birchwood "connector." *Based on a sketch by Arto Sverloff.*

metal tube that could be pounded into the bearing case in place of the broken piece. First he whittled a carefully shaped "connector" of birch and pounded it into the hollow end of the broken axle. By a stroke of unusual luck, one of his small ratchet wrench sockets fitted snugly over the birchwood shaft and, with a little hammering, he fitted it into the bearing case. Figure 3 illustrates the crucial repair that enabled Arto to drive his vehicle some fifteen kilometers back home.

The use of birchwood for repairs is particularly important in the event of broken skis or ski support springs. Although the skis on the front of snowmobiles are made of metal, their general shape and function immediately suggest the wooden skis that Lapps made and used for centuries. Improvised birchwood "skis" are quite functional for at least temporary repairs of broken snowmobiles.

Another example from Arto's experiences is useful for illustrating the kinds of repairs that are undertaken, often under difficult or dangerous conditions. He had been traveling with a border guard in the area of Isokivinokka (Big Rocky Point) hauling signs that were to be placed along the Norwegian border. Driving in darkness in a relatively unfamiliar location, they tumbled into a rocky pocket off the side of a small cliff. Since Arto was standing up on his machine, he fell free and was not injured, but the border guard, riding on the supply sled, fell forward into the motor cowling and broke his collarbone.

The border guard set out to walk to a cabin at Kolmisvaara, not far away. Arto dug out his machine and was able to start it. He followed the border guard almost up to the cabin, but the engine suddenly died. The difficulty proved to be a loose condenser wire. In this case the solution was simple. He poured gasoline onto some rags and used this fire to heat the end of a screwdriver which he then used to re-solder the condenser connection.

While the border guards took their injured companion to the doctor in Nuorgam, Arto headed back toward Sevettijärvi. About halfway home the machine quit again. This time the problem was a burned-out head gasket. Arto set out on skis toward a cabin located at Opukasjärvi on the Näätämö river.

(Snowmobilers nearly always carry skis with them when driving in the backlands.)

At the Opukasjärvi camp he found materials for making a temporary headgasket. Some sort of tin can appeared to be suitable as a headgasket substitute, so he skied back the four miles to his machine and cut the tin can into the proper fit with the cylinder head. The rest of the drive back to Sevettijärvi was uneventful.

Probably the height of innovativeness was reached by Niila Näkkäläjärvi of Vaskojoki, who built his own snowmobile. He used some spare parts from other snowmobiles, as well as parts of an old automobile. The most original feature of his machine was the steering mechanism, which consisted of a single wide ski on the front end, rather than the usual twin-ski arrangement. A few years after this striking instance of local initiative, one of the Swedish snowmobile manufacturers came out with a single-ski vehicle. (It has not been determined whether or not there is any connection between the two events.)

The Lapp snowmobile operator traveling in the backlands does not, of course, simply trust to luck or the presence of birchwood to keep his machine working. Most of the experienced men carry a variety of spare parts and repair equipment with them. For driving in search of reindeer or in other activities that might require several days in the woods, the well-equipped snowmobiler usually carries spare spark plugs, a spare "ski attachment rod," a selection of wrenches and screwdrivers, soldering equipment, a small bottle of wood alcohol (for deicing the fuel line), and a spare V-belt, as well as an extra can of gasoline. In addition to these items, the Lappish backwoodsman generally carries at least one, often two, sharp knives and an axe for fire building and other purposes.

Rope lassos are no longer used very much on reindeer, but the herdsmen usually carry them—for a new and different purpose. On those occasions when the machines get hung up in snowbanks or in watery traps (for example, locations of hidden warm springs under the snow), the lassos are used to pull them out of the mire. Lassos are, of course, handy for tying, securing, and a variety of other purposes.

Not everyone among the Lapps is a "natural born" mechanic. Mistakes in judgment and careless handling of the machines have taken a toll. For example, two young men from the Sevettijärvi community drove brand-new machines full-tilt from Kaamanen all the way to Sevettijärvi, severely damaging the motors before they were properly broken in. Two seasoned snowmobilers joked about the early days, when they were so naïve that they put oil on their drive belts, thinking that a little lubrication would improve performance. It is widely agreed that many of the worn-out machines that are adding to visual pollution in Lapland met their demise through carelessly rough usage.

Critics of local snowmobile maintenance standards point to the history of that very first machine in Lapland, the Partakko teacher's original Ski-Doo. As previously noted, that master mechanic took such loving care of his vehicle that it was still in excellent condition in 1971 when the Bombardier company bought it back from him.

There is a paradox involved in the picture I have presented, but I believe that the ostensible contradiction can be explained. The reindeer herdsmen (and other snowmobile users of northeastern Finland) appear to have very considerable capabilities in repairing damaged equipment. This does not, however, insure that they are *always* cautious and thoughtful in preserving and protecting the longevity of machines through effective maintenance techniques.

The relative success of the Lapps in maintaining and repairing their snowmobiles appears to be a consequence of their long-standing self-sufficiency in constructing and maintaining travel equipment, shelter, boats, fishing equipment, and other material items. In more recent times they have added technical skills through experience with repairing outboard motors, chain saws, bicycles, and other manufactured equipment.

In addition to this presence of a large store of experience with material things, the Lapp "pre-adaptation" to snowmobile technology appears to be enhanced by the egalitarian and individualistic structure of socioeconomic life in the region. The economic independence and physical separation of individual households has encouraged people to seek their own

Photo 3.   Lapps have been very successful in diagnosing mechanical problems and making repairs on their snowmobiles. *(Ludger Müller-Wille)*

solutions to technological problems through trial and error. In real life and in folktales Lapp protagonists are often faced with situations that require the invention of temporary substitutes or other technical solutions to meet material needs. In their idle hours the Lapps exchange stories about their various solutions to technical problems—of reindeer herding, finding their way in unfamiliar territory, and maintaining equipment. Nowadays these exchanges of "folklore" often revolve around technical features of their snowmobiles.

It should be noted that many of the skills that Lapps have developed in connection with the snowmobiles are relatively new; they are not simply transfers of old techniques from pre-snowmobile equipment to new materials. Their technical adaptiveness appears to depend to a great extent on certain attitudinal and psychological features—including the patience and attention to physical detail that makes it possible for the Lappish home mechanic to put his machine back together after he has taken it apart. There is, of course, much variation among the Lapps in their degree of patience, skills, and other qualities needed for successful and creative adaptation to this new age of mechanization.

Specialized Repair Facilities

The list of repairs on Arto Sverloff's Ski-Doo (given above) was affirmed by several people to be typical of their own experiences. "Of course, some people have more break-downs, others less. . . ." But, on the average, several hundred Finnmarks were required annually to pay repair bills, even though most of the work was carried out by the owners themselves. For extensive overhauling the snowmobiles had to be sent to Inari or Ivalo.

For the past few years, however, the Lasoff men have had their own welding equipment and have been able to repair broken front skis and other frequently encountered breakages. Also, three different local dealers have established the beginnings of repair facilities, particularly to service the machines carrying their sales guarantees. The leading storekeeper in Sevettijärvi was the first local person to become an agent for snow vehicle sales. He is now the agent for Evinrude machines, and his mechanic, a Skolt, repairs them, although they are not fully equipped for all types of repair work.

The local Ski-Doo agent, a tundra Lapp, employed a mechanic during the winter of 1970–71 who worked mainly on the Ski-Doos of the area that needed warranty repairs. Swedish machines are distributed locally from a new store very close to the Norwegian border. A local Skolt Lapp has worked occasionally for this agency servicing the new generation of these machines.

In large part, these three repair services are all devoted to maintaining new machines. Some Lapps have adopted the policy of trading in their machines at least every other year. This practice assures them that most repairs are paid for from the company warranties, rather than from their own cash reserves. People who cannot afford to purchase the new vehicles are still without comprehensive repair facilities. It would appear that such a shop in the Sevettijärvi area would have a lucrative business, since the rapidly growing number of local automobiles (as well as the transient tourist traffic) are also without repair services. The investment needed to establish such a facility is perhaps beyond the reach of most of the mechanically able men in the community, but the present Finnish policy of loans to small businesses could make such a commercial venture feasible.

Characteristics of Successful Machines and Styles of Use

The Bombardier Ski-Doo company's exclusive control of the Lapland market lasted only a short time. Competition from other manufacturers developed at least by the winter of 1964–65. In that year three Polaris Mustangs from the United States found their way into the Sevettijärvi area. Opinions differ somewhat on their effectiveness but the chief cause of their demise (in this region) was that spare parts were no longer available when the original dealers went out of business. In 1965–66 three or four Swedish Ockelbo machines were sold to local people, but they also failed to excite much enthusiasm, and very few models have been seen since then.

As we can see in Table 3, 1966–67 was a landmark year in the snowmobile revolution. At least sixteen persons acquired machines during that winter. The Lapp herdsmen claim that the large spurts in snowmobile acquisition in 1967 (and again in 1969) coincide with the appearance of machines that were particularly well-adapted to their requirements. Of course, the availability of investment cash played an important role in purchase patterns; on the other hand, the Lapps are quick to list the factors that identify their favorite machines.

The Swedish machine, Motoski, which was introduced in 1967, had a number of very desirable features. The excellent warranty covered most of the moving parts for a full year against all breakage, and the owner was even paid for his labor if he repaired the machine himself. In most respects the design of the Motoski did not differ greatly from that of the Ski-Doo;

Figure 4a.   Driving a snowmobile using the standing position. *Drawn by Seppo Sverloff, age 12.*

Figure 4b.   A snowmobile driver in the kneeling position, towing a sled of firewood. Drawn by Jorma Fofanoff.

however, the fifteen horsepower Sachs motor delivered greater power than had been available on the Ski-Doo or other lightweight machines.

The center of balance of the entire vehicle was in the middle—on the track, rather than on the front skis. This contrasts with some other machines that have a heavy front end, especially with forward fuel tanks. These forward-weighted machines tend to "dive" in deep snow and are almost useless in difficult terrain. Some machines have rather wide footboards which also tend to hang up in soft snow, preventing the drive track from sinking into full engagement with the snow under the machine.

The position of the seat is of great importance to the herders. Most snowmobile seats appear to be designed for sitting in a straddle position as on a motorcycle. This position is for tourists and playboys, say the Lapps. For effective driving in the backlands, particularly in tricky maneuvering with reindeer, there are two main options—standing up on the footboards or else kneeling on the seat in a sort of sidesaddle style (see Figure 4). Both the kneeling position and standing style are employed effectively in the Sevettijärvi area. Driving from a standing position insures maximum effectivenss in maneuvering. By placing himself well above the windshield, the driver can see obstacles and pick out alternative routes through the clusters of trees, scattered boulders, and other hazards that constantly threaten to trap his machine. At the same time, the standing driver can see reindeer in the distance and judge their movements.

Another important reason for the stand-up style of driving is much less apparent to the casual observer. Experienced herders report that steering in rough terrain is effected mainly by rocking from side to side, rather than simply turning the steering apparatus. In fact, they say, reliance on the steering apparatus is sure to result in breakage of the steering column, for it is not engineered to withstand the strains of maneuvering in rugged territory. Thus, the standing driver is constantly shifting his weight to one side or the other in virtually automatic reactions to small nuances in the terrain.

(Mitri Semenoff suggested that, because of these facts concerning driving style, a machine with a single frontal ski, such as is now featured on one of the new Ockelbo models, would be more effective than the twin-ski system of front suspension.)

Pleasure drivers on the snowmobile trails of North America would be interested in still another reason the Lapps give for their driving style. Both the kneeling and standing positions give them personal mobility for avoiding accidents and also for absorbing shocks from sharp bumps and free falls. Every herdsman occasionally drives off small ridges or even real cliffs in his pursuit of reindeer in the darkness and reduced visibility of the arctic winter. The motorized reindeer herder places himself in a position in which these jolts and jars are absorbed by arms, legs, and thighs, rather than the base of his spine. Reports of snowmobile injuries from Wisconsin and Minnesota include a serious increase in spinal injuries; the styles of driving adopted by the Lapps may indeed be important in reducing accidents as they claim.

As we suggested earlier, the Lapps are convinced that much of snowmobile engineering and design is adapted for a recreational use rather than for the functional purposes they see as paramount. The seat of many snowmobiles is often at the wrong height, from their point of view, and one otherwise quite effective machine even had a slanted seat arrangement which would have caused the kneeling Lappish driver to slide forward into his motor cockpit!

Certainly, snowmobile design appears to be insensitive to the kinds of uses that Lapps find to be most important. However, the special ways that Lapps have adjusted to them reflects, in part, the fact that the Lapps are generally quite lightly built. Although they tend to be strong, average weights of the Skolt Lapp men are considerably less than the populations who are the main purchasers of snow vehicles.

After the early period of trial and error in selecting machines that would be effective in reindeer herding and other rough-terrain usage, Lapps appear to have developed some very clear notions of effective engineering design and make their purchases accordingly. Differences in snowmobile preferences that seem to be matters of personal taste or whim have turned out, on closer inspection, to reflect significant differences in the use patterns and adaptive strategies of different households.

Two Snowmobiles: The Basic Unit of Effectiveness

Although most men expect to be able to keep their own equipment operating satisfactorily, it has become usual for reindeer herdsmen and other backland travelers to drive in pairs. This improves communications (one person can drive back to the settlements with information about the herds, while the other continues the work). But the major explanation for this pattern is the concern for safety. In case of accident, motor trouble, or any other kind of emergency the second machine is available to carry the men back home.

The team approach is also directly useful in herding operations. The men have found that two collaborating snowmobiles constitute a kind of "minimal effective unit" for driving reindeer, especially if the terrain is somewhat rough. When one snowmobile attempts to drive a group of reindeer in a particular direction, the animals can easily circle back; two machines, one on either side of the herd, can force the animals in a particular direction.

Many Skolt Lapps experience periods of enforced idleness while waiting for their machines to be returned from repairs in Inari or Rovaniemi. Sometimes their machines sit idle while the operator waits for replacement parts that he has ordered. Such periods of breakdown constitute serious threats to economic success. A spare snowmobile would seem a natural solution to this problem, but that costs a lot of money. A few of the wealthier households have two machines, even in cases in which there is only one main active driver. Jakkima Osipov has two machines, one of which is not particularly suited to reindeer herding but which can be taken out into the woods if his lighter machine needs repairs. Arto Sverloff has two Evinrudes, neither of which is particularly suited to reindeer herding; and in the winter of 1970–71 he played a relatively small role in reindeer activities, since he was under contract to haul firewood to the school. For one of his machines he purchased an extension track to increase its load-pulling capacity. Much of the winter was devoted to wood hauling, for which his specially adapted machine was ideal. His wife used the other machine to drive to school every morning, where she worked as an assistant cook. The smaller machine was used, therefore, as a general transportation vehicle—for trips to reindeer roundups, occasional participation in gathering reindeer as well as for recreational use. However, Arto's transportation system is complicated by the fact that he also has an automobile.

In most cases the presence of more than one machine in the household reflects the fact that there is more than one active male adult in the family. There appears to be only one household in which a second snowmobile is maintained solely because of the wife's driving activities. In this case the wife, who is childless, has always taken a prominent part in herding activities and travels extensively with her husband in the backlands.

Summary and Conclusions

Lappish reindeer herders adapted rather quickly to the technical demands of the snowmobile. They readily transferred their skills in routine motor repair and maintenance from previous experience with outboard motors, motorbikes, and chain saws. Most snowmobile owners attempt to repair their own equipment, but some men are more expert than others in these matters. For larger repairs, such as rebuilding burned-out motors, the men have had to rely on services located outside the local community, although some specialized repair facilities are now becoming available. The neighboring Utsjoki community already has a fully equipped repair shop. Thus, the new occupational specialization of providing machine repair service is developing in northeastern Lapland, just as it has in areas of increased automobile use.

Some of the maintenance difficulties and other engineering problems that the Lapps experience with snowmobiles could be eliminated if manufacturers made a careful study of the special technical requirements involved in heavy backland use of snowmobiles. Apparently some efforts in this direction, particularly among the Swedish manufacturers of snow vehicles, have already been instituted. Perhaps the single most significant change in the economics of snowmobile maintenance has been the development of effective full-year warranties on the machines. Certainly there has been a sharp decline in total maintenance costs—for those Lapps who can afford to buy the newer models.

CHAPTER SEVEN

The Mechanization
of Reindeer Herding:
Disaster for the Skolt Lapps

Thus far the picture I have presented concerning the adoption of snowmobiles in Sevettijärvi (and other areas of Lapland) has a rather positive tone. Early experiences with the machines demonstrated their wide-ranging usefulness; they even seemed to be highly effective in reindeer herding; and the Lapps and their neighbors apparently have been quite skillful in managing repair and maintenance problems. All of the early signs suggested that the use of snowmobiles in reindeer herding would be highly successful; in fact, as I have pointed out in Chapter Five, herders all over Lapland were quick to mechanize their herding operations. Evidently many herdsmen felt that this modernization would make herding physically easier and economically more advantageous.

On the other hand, the tone of Arto Sverloff's letter (quoted on page 69) certainly suggested that all was not well in reindeer operations around Sevettijärvi. Interviews with Skolt Lapps and others during the spring of 1967 revealed a deep division of opinion among herdsmen concerning the use of snowmobiles in herding. Clearly, the transition to mechanized reindeer husbandry was not working out well for at least a portion of the community.

Those earlier forebodings were, in my opinion, fully justified. The chain of events brought about by the snowmobile, exacerbated by other factors, led to progressive deterioration of the reindeer-herding situation for the Skolt Lapps in the Mud-dusjärvi association. By 1971 some of the main dimensions of this reindeer disaster were clear.

1. The total number of reindeer owned by Skolts in the association had dropped precipitously, from a high of over 2600 in 1960–61 to below 1700 in the spring of 1971.

2. This decline in total herd size does not accurately portray the seriousness of the situation, however, for *one family* now owned nearly one third of the reindeer, while nearly all the rest had suffered serious losses. Average family herd size was down from about fifty to just twelve reindeer.

3. Two thirds of the Skolt families in the association were for practical purposes eliminated from reindeer keeping, since their herds were now too small to be economically significant.

4. A large proportion of the men who had been active herdsmen in 1960 had dropped out of herding activities almost entirely. Some had found wage-labor employment; others were now officially and literally unemployed.

5. In the new herding system, developed in the period 1967–71, there are no longer any winter herds and no spring calving operations. Owners have access to their reindeer only during roundups. Most families, even those without snowmobiles, cannot maintain draught animals for hauling. They must hire transportation from the snowmobilers or from automobiles.

The causes of these developments are very complicated, and it appears that the snowmobile technology was a necessary, but not sufficient, factor in the process. Aspects of both the physical and social environment also had a part in the outcome. I will first take up what seem to be direct effects of the machines on the man-reindeer interaction system before turning to the examination of economic, political, and social ramifications.

De-domestication of the Herds

One of the primary effects of the snowmobile is a progressive "de-domestication" of the reindeer herds. In effect, the animals have been allowed to return to a near-wild stage. Relinquishing control over the animals represents the continuation of a trend that was already evident before the coming of the snowmobile. The use of snowmobiles pushed the dedomestication process to its logical, and possibly irreversible, limits.

As noted earlier, the transition from Suenjel to Sevettijärvi marked a shift in the degree of control that the Skolt Lapps had over their animals. The intensive herding practices of the Suenjel days produced animals that were quite "tame" and relatively easy to manage. The high degree of control is perhaps best epitomized by the fact that it was possible to tie up and milk reindeer cows, even during the October mating season when they were most excitable. In those prewar days the men had "custody" of their reindeer from October to June.

The reduction in family control after World War II came about because of both social and environmental factors. The loss of the tame old Suenjel reindeer required the establishment of totally new herds with animals that lacked the "social tradition" of intense interaction with their masters in relatively small-scale territorial bounds. The importance of the Finnish association system also played its part, together with special features of the Sevettijärvi landscape.

The decline in degree of control that characterized presnowmobile herding in Sevettijärvi was seen by the Skolts as one of the major causes for the problems of the 1950s and early 1960s. Nevertheless, reindeer men had custody of a major portion of their herds throughout the last half of the winter, enabling them to tie the cows for the all-important spring calving. It provided the best system for insuring that calves were earmarked, and a successful spring calving certainly gave the herder a feeling of control over the destinies of his reindeer, even though summer predators, disease, and other accidents always took some toll of the newborn animals. At least the calves that lived through their first months did not fatten the herds of those active and conscienceless men who sought to claim every unmarked calf for their own.

In pre-snowmobile days gathering herds was a leisurely process, often lasting several weeks. As larger and larger numbers of animals were accumulated, a social system developed

Photo 4. The reindeer are collected into large groups and driven by the snowmobiles to the roundup. *(Jorg Trobitzsch)*

in which the animals became accustomed to one another and to the men and their dogs. Most of the interaction between men and their animals was relatively peaceful, and the herdsmen even aided the reindeer in the winter food quest by searching out new grazing areas in the deep snow.

This picture of "peaceful coexistence" was abruptly altered when snowmobiles came into extensive use. The tone of herd control changed—the animals were frequently chased, sometimes for rather long distances, and contacts between men and animals were lessened since the men no longer spent weeks and months in gathering and living with the herds. Partly because of the high costs of motor operation, they sought to sweep the herds together in a few days, transporting them toward roundup sites with a minimum of delay. The quickly gathered herds were no longer in any sense "social systems," but simply bunches of frightened animals forced to run in the same direction. It is highly likely that the noise and smell of the machines also added to the growing unruliness of the reindeer.

As relationships between men and animals continued to deteriorate, many of the scattered clusters of reindeer began to seek refuge in the more inaccessible (rockier and brushier) pockets of the region. The reindeer were gradually changing their living habits; they appeared to be seeking escape from the strains and annoyances brought by the machines.

There is an opposing view of these developments. According to the advocates of the snowmobile, the disorganized behavior of the reindeer in the early middle part of the 1960s was brought about by deterioration in lichen conditions. Furthermore, the failures in herd management during these experimental years were due to inexperience and carelessness among the drivers. Thus, they argue, the gradual accumulation of expertise by the most experienced and able snowmobile men would restore order if given a chance.

The de-domestication of the reindeer herds in the Sevettijärvi region did not, of course, happen over night. The process continued over a period of several years, with certain crucial feedback mechanisms that pushed the system well beyond the expectations of the Lapp herders. When the herdsmen of the Muddusjärvi reindeer district first started using snowmobiles, their intention was simply to substitute a much swifter and easier means of transportation for the traditional, tediously slow, reindeer sleds and skis. They had no intention of changing the basic organization of reindeer herding.

The complex interconnectedness of herder-and-reindeer relationships can be seen most clearly in some of the events of the Muddusjärvi herding cycle as they were played out during the "transitional years" of 1964–67. The main roundup at the Tsiuttijoki corral in the winter of 1965, for example, was particularly memorable in that it was planned and organized in terms of the long-standing practices and schedules of the pre-snowmobile era, and was turned to chaos because of the now recalcitrant reindeer. The first fruits of the de-domestication process were apparent to everyone. Arto Sverloff described some of the confusion as follows:

> ... when the main roundup was announced it just went on and on ... and they held recess periods, and then continued ... it stretched out for perhaps a month, that one roundup ... at first they got quite a few head, but the later part was a sort of messing around ... they couldn't seem to get them, but the roundup continued anyway ... reindeer were brought a few at a time. ...

In earlier times the activities at the roundup corral were usually completed in a week or less, even if there were a couple of "rest days." In the situation Arto described, the reindeer owners waited impatiently around the roundup site for several weeks while the snowmobile men made sweep after sweep through the backlands, with steadily diminishing effectiveness in bringing animals to the enclosure.

Out of this chaos the herders sought to bring order through the usual means, by transporting their captured animals to home pastures for winter herding. But the fact that the roundup had been very incomplete, with many small groups of reindeer still scattered around in the region, had further serious consequences.

Reindeer herds, especially those that have been under considerable human control, display a balance of centripetal and centrifugal tendencies in which the centripetal force is approximately proportional to the number of animals. Large herds tend to maintain their integrity, and they attract additional reindeer that stray into their "orbit." Small herds tend to disperse because of insufficient "pull." Transporting small herds through areas in which there are many stray reindeer is therefore jeopardized by both internal and external forces.

When the Skolt herdsmen attempted to drive their badly depleted collection of animals home from the Tsiuttijoki roundup, their little herd mixed with the free-roaming intransigents that had escaped the roundup altogether. After a great deal of effort a remnant of the Sevettijärvi winter herd was finally brought to the home pasture area, but the winter of

1965 was the last time they were able to get even a small number of reindeer under their control. The neat and orderly progression from association roundups to owner-controlled winter herding groups was no longer possible.

For the Skolts the loss of the winter herds was a blow of major proportions. It automatically eliminated any possibility of spring calving operations, and it also ended the time-honored security system based on maintaining one's own (however small) store of food and negotiable assets in nearby pasturelands. A few people still managed to tie a small number of cows for calving in the spring of 1965, but after that all semblance of the old reindeer system was gone.

By 1967 the general strategy of association roundups had been drastically revised in an attempt to regain a measure of organization in the still-deteriorating situation. Roundups were now called on short notice (the speed of the snowmobiles would insure that people could get to them in time), and they usually involved small herds, gathered in a few days of intensive combing of a prescribed area. Attempts to gather a "north herd" and "south herd" had been abandoned completely. Some of the roundups were staged in quite temporary enclosures, constructed of a few hundred meters of burlap "fencing." This innovation had come into use in nearby areas in the mid-1960s and was seen as an exceedingly fortunate way of coping with the fact that it was becoming increasingly difficult to drive the reindeer from out-of-the-way areas to the permanent roundup locations.

In April 1967 I took part in a small roundup in an area on the boundary between the Muddusjärvi and Vätsäri districts. Since this took place during the transitional period, there were still some elements of pre-snowmobile days. At the same time, the events in this roundup highlight some of the main features and complexities of the new situation. After the burlap enclosure had been hastily erected, several dozen herders hid along the sides of a narrow lake that was to be the approach to the enclosure. They formed a human funnel fence, aided by natural features of the landscape. The herd was led by a ski-man leading a bell-reindeer, just as in "the old days." Ski-men also patrolled the flanks. Snowmobiles brought up the rear.

Figure 5. In the "old style" of herding, reindeer were led single file into a corral by ski-men and a bell-reindeer. Hidden ski-men wait to prevent animals from escaping.

Near the entrance to the enclosure the herd of about 300 animals bolted, with the snowmobiles in quick but fruitless pursuit. The reindeer easily eluded the machines in the pine forest. The machines were not blamed for the failure in this instance, but some herders commented that the animals are so wild nowadays that such failures are to be expected.

The next morning the herd was again located and made ready for a drive to the corral. This time the burlap enclosure was erected in a thick grove near the shore of the large lake Tsuolisjärvi. The expanse of ice would provide a wide-open field for the deployment of snowmobiles. Once again a *laidis-taja*—the ski-man with bell-reindeer—started toward the enclosure. The herders hid along the edge of the lake (see Figure 5), waiting to close the trap when the animals had been lured or driven into the fence. As the lead reindeer approached the trap the herd began to scatter in several directions at once. But each little rebel group of reindeer was turned back to the line of march by the swiftly moving machines. They had no place to go but forward—into the trap. The skier with his bell-reindeer brought up the rear. This was one of the last times that a *laidistaja* was used, for it had become apparent that the animals *cannot be led* into the roundup enclosure—they must be driven.

In this little roundup at Tsuolisjärvi there were no meat buyers, but some unclaimed animals were auctioned off to individual herders. A few men butchered animals for home consumption, and a few calves were earmarked. Adult animals were tallied to the lists of their respective owners, and then the entire herd was turned loose again. It was late afternoon when the men headed for home. One of the striking indicators of the snowmobile revolution was the presence, at this roundup, of a herdsman from Partakko, some sixty kilometers to the southwest. In an earlier day it would have taken him two days to get there and it is unlikely he would have come, but now it was a matter of only a few hours.

Some of the main features of the new reindeer-herding situation evident in this roundup include the following:

1. The herd to be "processed" was rather small and had been gathered on fairly short notice.

2. Both snowmobiles and ski-men were involved in the action, because of the rough and woody terrain.

3. The failure of the first day's attempt to corral the animals may have been due to a general increase in suspiciousness and caution among the animals. In any case, the animals refused to be *led* into a corral.

4. In the action of the following day, the animals again bolted, giving further evidence of their general wariness and lack of trust in humans.

5. On the flat surface of the lake ice the snowmobiles could, indeed, outmaneuver the reindeer, and the use of a *laidistaja* (lead reindeer) proved to be an almost meaningless complication in the action.

6. The animals were released into the forest after two or three hours of roping activity. Thus, the reindeers' total interaction with humans consisted of a few days of being driven into a cluster, plus a day and a half of frightening chase and capture. If the herdsmen had wanted to take animals home to "winter herds," it would not have been possible.

7. Some of the animals caught up in this sweep had already been captured in roundups held earlier during the winter. Since winter herds are not maintained, any particular group of reindeer always includes some "processed" and some "unprocessed" animals.

The developing wildness of the reindeer required, of course, suitable countermeasures on the part of the herders. The annual herding cycle as practiced by the Skolt Lapps in 1970–71 demonstrates the strategy and tactics that had been worked out in an attempt to reestablish a "working relationship" with the now quite wild reindeer.

In the middle of November a group of nine herders with two supporting snowmobiles set out to the southwest end of the district to begin gathering animals in the direction of the Ahvenjärvi reindeer corral (see Map 6). The area labeled A in Map 6 was combed by men on foot, with the two snowmobiles carrying supplies and occasionally aiding in actual herding operations. About ten centimeters of snow had fallen, which was not enough to permit much maneuvering with the machines, and even skis were relatively useless. The men worked their

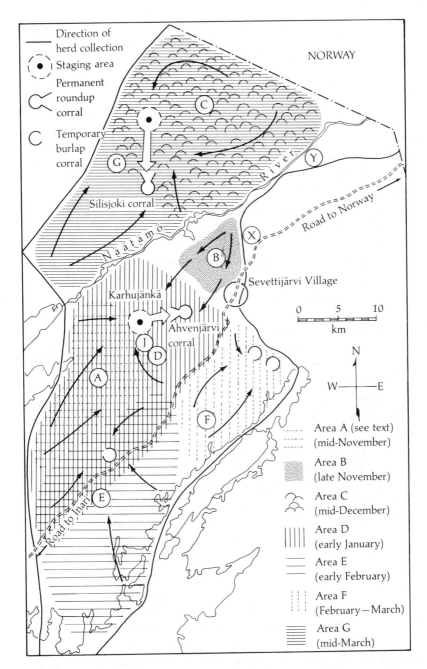

Map 6.   Areas of reindeer collection operations in Näätämö association, 1970–71.

way on foot toward the northeast, to approximately point J when the herds scattered and the herders were unable to maintain control because of their poor mobility.

After this first failure the herdsmen waited about a week for better weather before setting out again. This time one group returned to approximately the same starting point, in the southwest, while a second group (four men) drove to Jänisjärvi (point X on Map 6) to begin gathering the animals that were in the region between Sevettijärvi and the Näätämö River. This is a somewhat rocky area, mostly open tundra with only patches of pine forest. The men left their snowmobiles at points X and Y respectively, from which they set out on skis to circle behind the animals and drive them toward the west. At the end of each day the herders returned to the snowmobiles and drove home for the night. Each day at least a part of the group ski'd back into the area that had been cleared in order to make sure that the animals had not drifted back into the northeast corner.

After four days of pressing the reindeer westward the men had more or less cleared area B of reindeer, and met the group from the west, who were bringing up their herd from area A. Still operating mainly on skis, they pressed the herds into the general area of Karhujänkä ("Bear Swamp") which is the usual staging area for moving herds to the Ahvenjärvi roundup enclosure.

On December 8 the herd was driven, under tight snowmobile control, from Karhujänkä to the roundup enclosure. Six snowmobiles participated in the final drive. Figure 6, based on drawings by two of the participants in this roundup, shows the general strategy employed in driving the animals to the corral. Two machines were at the vanguard, pointing the herd into the "trap"; two machines operated as flankers, and a pair of machines brought up the rear, keeping a constant pressure on the animals. This "forced march" system of driving the herd into the enclosure was carried out at a brisk pace, with most of the animals keeping up a steady trot. It is significant to note that the ski-men who were active in earlier stages of the operations do not usually have an opportunity to participate in the final drive to the corral under this new system.

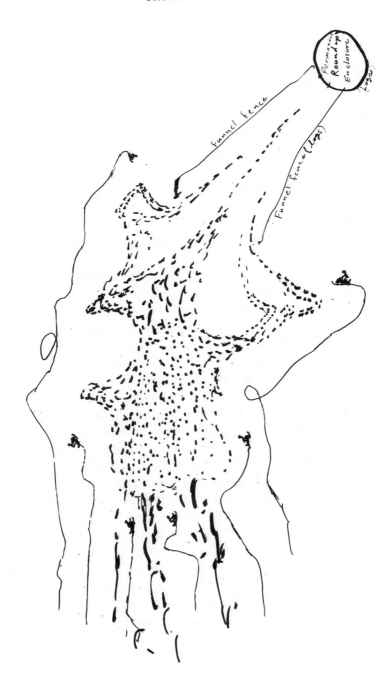

Figure 6. In reindeer work with snowmobiles, herds must be driven rather than led. This drawing by Arto Sverloff shows six snowmobile men driving a large herd of reindeer into a roundup corral.

The second day of the roundup (December 9) was devoted to numbering calves for identification purposes, and the final day was spent in roping and marking calves and other animals. Under the new system of contract herding, the men who participated in the drive were to be paid on the basis of the total number of adult reindeer actually brought to the corral, instead of receiving a fixed daily wage. The rate for 1970–71 was eight Finnmarks (two dollars) per animal. Since the herders, through their collective efforts, brought in 478 animals (not including calves), they had a total of 3864 Finnmarks to divide in terms of fifty-five man-days of work. In the settlement the men with snowmobiles were paid at the rate of seventy marks per day, and ski-men received thirty-five marks per day for their work in this roundup.

Shortly after the first roundup was completed, a group of six snowmobilers and one skier drove up into the northeastern corner of the district (area C on Map 6) and combed that area, bringing a total of 300 to 400 reindeers to the Silisjoki enclosure for a roundup that took place December 18-20.

The third roundup of the season was scheduled for early January. Seven snowmobile men and five or six ski-men moved through area D (Map 6), which overlaps extensively with the area that had been covered in the first roundup. This time approximately 300 animals were brought to the Ahven-järvi corral. The snow cover had increased substantially during December, so that the men were able to carry out the major part of this roundup with machines. Ski-men worked in the forested and rocky area in the south of area D, attempting to force the reindeer to travel north into more open territory, but they evidently had little success. Herding activities in that area have continued to be a source of irritation between ski-men and snowmobilers. The latter claim that these operations prove that ski-men are relatively worthless in modern herding, while the nonmechanized herdsmen blame the machines for making the animals so wild that they hide in the forest and refuse to be herded.

The rocky and forested areas in the southwest (see Map 7) were again combed by ski-men for a few days in early February, resulting in a roundup on February 9, 10, 11 with

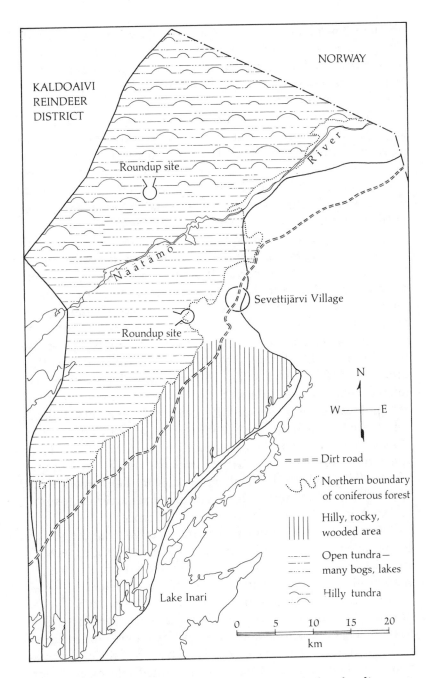

KALDOAIVI
REINDEER
DISTRICT

NORWAY

Roundup site

River

Näätämö

Sevettijärvi Village

Roundup site

N

W ———— E

=== = Dirt road

Northern boundary
of coniferous forest

Hilly, rocky,
wooded area

Open tundra—
many bogs, lakes

Hilly tundra

Lake Inari

0   5   10   15   20

km

Map 7.   Terrain of the Näätämö association reindeer-herding area.

about 100 head. Once again the true effectiveness of the herding procedures remains an open question, with arguments
among the reindeer men as to whether most of the reindeer of
that area remained uncollected and unmarked in spite of the
efforts of the ski-men.

In the latter part of February, the rugged terrain in the
southern corner of the region along the north shore of Lake
Inari was similarly combed, with mixed results, by men on
skis. On February 24 they got about eighty reindeer into the
enclosure, and then on March 11 approximately 100 animals
were captured. These events are clear indicators of the piece-
meal nature of the entire herding cycle nowadays.

The roundups at Jorvapuolijärvi and Vaasiliselkä were
carried out using temporary burlap enclosures. Since neither of
these areas has a fixed corral, it would have been impossible
to hold a roundup in those areas in earlier years. The principles
which account for the success of the burlap roundup corral
were incorporated in an innovation that extended the approach
fence for several kilometers, in a fashion reminiscent of the
techniques used by hunters to drive buffalo, caribou, and other
prey into pitfalls, "cliff-falls," or other traps. Lightweight ny-
lon cord with plastic ribbons tied at one to two meter intervals
are stretched out for several kilometers to form a "psychological barrier" which reindeer will usually avoid approaching.
This temporary "fence" is extended in the form of a V from
the mouth of the temporary burlap enclosure, providing a
"funnel" into which the reindeer are driven. The same kind of
"fence" is used in conjunction with fixed reindeer enclosures,
as extensions of the permanent "funnel fences."

As can be seen from the examples above, roundups with
temporary enclosures of burlap (plus cord and ribbons) tend to
be quite small, and represent "mop-up operations" carried out
mainly after larger roundups have been completed.

The final roundup of the 1970–71 season took place in the
northern part of the district, above Näätämö River (area G in
Map 6). This operation was carried out by snowmobile, culmi-
nating in a roundup at the end of March at the Silisjoki permanent corral. About 400 animals were tallied. No meat buyers

came to this roundup since the quality of the reindeer meat and the weight of the animals had dropped substantially by that time. It is very poor practice, economically, to slaughter animals in the later winter months, and meat buyers are increasingly concentrating their buying into the period from September to January.

The reindeer that were captured and tallied in these operations (five or six roundups) were mostly animals from neighboring associations. On the other hand, these neighboring associations also captured a number of animals for the Skolt Lapps in their roundups. The total number of adult reindeer realized by the Skolts from all these roundups came to 1689 plus 310 calves—a figure well below the tallied herds at the beginning of the 1960s.

When the roundups had all been held, the winter cycle of reindeer herding was finished, for there could be no spring calving. However, the Skolts, like their neighbors in other associations, are attempting to compensate for the loss of control over their calves through the practice of summer calf-marking. This is a system that has been in use for a number of years in other parts of Lapland and was developed from the extensive herding systems of the western and northern Lapps. At about midsummer the reindeer are generally found in large herds as a defensive response to the plagues of insects, so it is relatively easy to drive them into enclosures. In former times the little calves (then only about five to six weeks old) were caught with lassos, but a new technological device—a long hoop—has been developed by Finnish herders in south Lapland for use in catching the fleet-footed little animals. Since the calves are very young they tend to follow their mothers quite closely, thus maximizing the possibility of correct owner identification (based on the owner marks on the ears of the mother).

The practice of summer marking is quite new in the Sevettijärvi area, but it may help to bring about a reversal in the serious decline in calf identification that has occurred. There are some negative factors to summer calf-marking, however. It appears that the confusion and running in the roundup enclosure is physically very hard on the young calves, so that a number of them die during this activity. It remains to be seen whether measures can be taken to make these sessions less strenuous for the reindeer.

By this time the reader may wonder whether the draught animals are kept around at least for emergencies. Unfortunately the process of de-domestication has made it nearly impossible to keep geldings. Among the reasons Skolts give for this development are the following:

1. Since the woods are now always full of wild reindeer, the special grazing areas reserved for geldings cannot be protected. The herds have decimated these areas.

2. Very few herdsmen went out during the fall to capture the geldings, so most of them remained with the (wild) herds. Those geldings that turned up in the roundups were, of course, not available until December-January at the earliest, long after they were needed.

3. Since nearly everyone has experienced increased cash needs, the relatively docile and heavy geldings were the most likely candidates for sale to meat buyers.

Maxim Osipoff told me that he kept a few geldings until 1968–69, but he finally quit when one of them died, apparently from starvation. On the other hand, Tatjana Prokoff still drove with a reindeer sled in the winter of 1970–71, although the family has a snowmobile.

Effects of Physical Harassment

While some of the disastrous decline in the Skolt Lapp herds has come about because of the direct and indirect effects of de-domestication, it is quite possible that the snowmobiles have had detrimental effects on the reindeer in yet another way. The opponents of snowmobile herding frequently claim that the animals are suffering physical damage from being driven too hard; continual harassment by those noisy machines also causes damage. Medical specialists who have examined slaughtered reindeer in the Näätämö area have apparently found some evidence of lung damage possibly caused by excessive running, but systematic evidence has not yet been collected in sufficient quantity to substantiate these claims. There are two sources of indirect evidence that suggest there is some substance to the charges.

The Norwegian meat buyer who purchases large numbers of reindeer in the Sevettijärvi region has stated that the average weight of the animals is now significantly lower than it was in pre-snowmobile days. In his experience, the two-year-old bulls averaged thirty-one to thirty-two kilograms in earlier years, but now the same type of animal weighs only twenty-five to twenty-six kilograms. Since this commercial operator's livelihood depends on a careful assessment of reindeer and their condition, his statements carry special weight. On the other hand, he does not keep detailed records, animal by animal, of his dealings, so the information remains suggestive but inconclusive.

A related source of indirect information about the health of reindeer herds is contained in the figures on calf production. These figures are available from the reindeer associations, who must relay their annual tallies of adult reindeer (by type) and numbers of calves to the central union of associations in Rovaniemi (Paliskuntain Yhdistys). The graph of "calf productivity" in Figure 7 is based on the official record of the Paliskuntain Yhdistys.

The figures on percentages of calves born show that over the years the annual natural increase in herds for all of Finnish Lapland has averaged about thirty percent. That is, the number of new calves in a given year tends to be about thirty percent of the total number of adult reindeer tallied. During the pre-snowmobile years the figures available for Lapland as a whole show that the northernmost associations—Kaldoaivi, Paistunturi and Muddusjärvi—tended to have a rate of calf production somewhat higher than the Lapland average. During the transitional period, in 1963–65, the average for those associations dropped to par with the rest of Lapland; since that time these mechanized reindeer herdsmen of the northeast corner have, for the most part, had rates of calf production *markedly below* the Lapland averages. This is, of course, only circumstantial

Photo 5. Within the roundup enclosure, each reindeer must be roped from the running herd and tallied before being removed. *(author)*

evidence. It does, however, suggest the possibility that snow-mobiles are somehow adversely affecting the number of viable calves added to the herds.

If these data are truly an indication of detrimental effects on calves, how does it come about? The behavior and physical characteristics of reindeer are a complex system, so we must expect that several different factors could be operating to produce health problems among the animals. The most direct explanation, however, focuses on the physiological stress experienced by females during the terminal months of pregnancy.

Mating season for reindeer is in the late fall, and most of the calves are born in the month of May, although there are always a few "summer calves." The adaptive logic of this time-table is that calves are born at a time when they will have full advantage of the summer season of abundant food, when reindeer graze and browse on grass, green leaves, and a variety of other vegetation. While the survival chances are thus maxi-

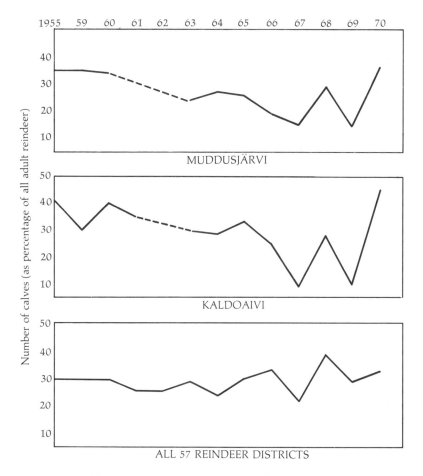

Figure 7. Calf productivity of a reindeer herd is a measure of its vitality. These graphs show the percentage of calves during the years of the "snowmobile revolution." *Compiled from annual reports published in* Poromies *(The Reindeer Man).* Some missing data in 1960, 1961, 1962.

mized for the newborn calves, this schedule puts a heavy strain on the pregnant females, for the most serious food shortages (which frequently result in the death of some of the animals) come in late winter. When lichens, the chief winter food, are buried under deep snows, reindeer must expend considerable energy in digging through the snow cover to feed themselves.

Ice formation, caused by alternate thawing and freezing, can make the situation much worse, especially if an ice crust forms directly over the lichen. In winters, when these serious obstacles to food-getting develop, the reindeer scatter widely, desperately searching for sheltered areas where they can still dig through to the lichen. Herding operations disturb the reindeer food-getting activities, forcing them to gather into larger aggregates in which grazing can become very difficult.

A more critical problem is the frightened running which takes place in the roundup enclosures. Often several hundred animals are running in the football-field sized oval while fifty to eighty men throw at them with lassos. The work goes on for hours before all the reindeer have been caught, tallied, and removed from the wild scene. "Time out" periods are called at frequent intervals, but the impatient reindeer men are quick to resume the action. It is widely assumed among reindeer herders that the activities in the corral constitute a serious physical torturing of the animals. Some new methods of processing reindeer without recourse to lassos have been developed, but these methods do not entirely eliminate the frightened running that characterizes the reindeer roundup.

The strains caused by gathering the animals into large herds, away from their "natural" feeding areas, and by the roundup itself were, of course, present in pre-snowmobile days. However, mechanized herding tactics have added significantly to the problems. Previously, the march from the "staging area" to the corral was carried out at a walking pace; now the snowmobiles force the panicked animals to run, often for several miles. What is probably more serious is that, under the new herding system, pregnant cows can experience this forced run and the roundup more than once. In pre-snowmobile days when the animals processed in a roundup were taken to home pastures for the rest of the winter, each animal had to endure the tortures of the roundup only once. Under the new conditions, in which the animals are turned loose after each roundup, many of them may be caught up in the gathering operations more than once during the winter. Since the typical pattern now includes five or six roundups in each district, there is a very considerable risk that a portion of the herds suffer

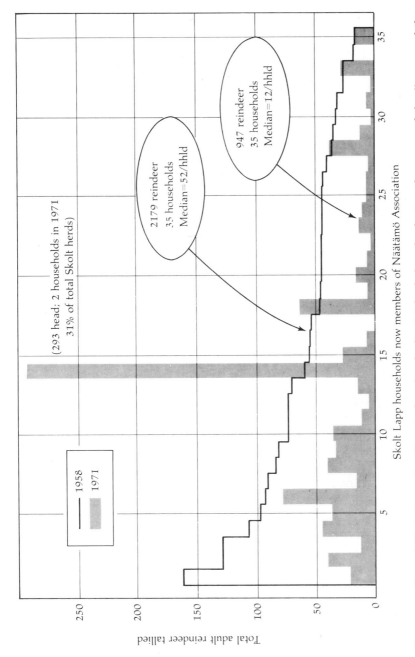

Figure 8. Size of Skolt Lapp family reindeer herds diminished sharply during the years of the "snowmobile revolution." This graph compares family herds in 1958 and 1971 for the 35 Skolt households in the Näätämö association. Four of these units include more than one nuclear family.

repeated strains from the roundup activities. Finally, it should be noted that the last roundups of the season have been occurring as late as the end of March or even in April, at a time when the cows are in their terminal months of pregnancy.

Under the present system, then, a portion of the pregnant females are suffering serious physical strain in repeated roundups, and there is, therefore, considerable possibility of some increases in calf mortality. The decline in the percentages of calves may be, in part, a reflection of this maladaptive aspect of mechanized reindeer herding.

Although the de-domestication of herds, coupled with the possible direct physical damage to the reindeer, are significant factors in the Sevettijärvi reindeer "disaster," these processes do not fully account for the severity of the Skolt losses; and they do not explain the fact that some individuals and families had to drop out of reindeer herding (see Figure 8). In order to understand these further developments we must turn to the economics of snowmobile ownership, and we must also look into the internal workings of the Muddusjärvi reindeer association.

Summary and Conclusions

The quality and character of life in Sevettijärvi has been profoundly changed during the 1960s—the decade of mechanization. Statistics about the size of reindeer herds and the costs of snowmobile upkeep cannot convey the ways in which a modern tone of hurry and frustration has become prevalent, along with a greatly heightened awareness of the "world outside." In some ways these changes of the past ten years have accomplished transformations analogous to the processes of change that went on for thirty or forty years after automobiles were introduced in the United States.

A whole complex of behaviors associated with the reindeer have been eliminated, and the loud sounds of gasoline motors have become regular and accepted features of the environment. The number of tourists visiting the area has increased many times over, and a large number of the "relics" of pre-snowmobile days have been sold to affluent visitors from the south. In terms of some indices of social change, the decade of the sixties has been even more dramatic than the traumatic forties.

Many of the changes can be regarded as progress by both local people and outside observers. The increases in communication and transportation have greatly accelerated the speed of medical services, for example, and there is now a much enlarged range of food available in the stores. The growth of commercial enterprises in the Sevettijärvi region now provides the people with a greater series of options in shopping for food and other necessities.

On the other hand, many of the changes brought by this technological and economic "modernization" give rise to a deep ambivalence, as well as concern about the future.

CHAPTER EIGHT

Economic and Political Consequences of Mechanized Herding

The Muddusjärvi reindeer association and its internal politics had a strong influence on the way in which the snowmobile revolution affected the Skolt Lapps. Throughout the 1950s and 1960s the Skolts were involved in a deepening conflict with the Finns and Lapps living in the western part of the district. The people around Sevettijärvi frequently talked of the need for a separate Skolt Lapp district. The other reindeer men in the association were for the most part strongly opposed to establishing a separate district, since it would in all probability mean a reduction of grazing area for their reindeer.

The conflicts between the Skolts and the westerners appear to have developed from their quite different ecological situations, influenced in part by their different perspectives on reindeer-herding techniques. As noted earlier, the Skolts had tried to maintain intensive control of their animals, partly because a large portion of their subsistence was dependent on reindeer. The westerners, on the other hand, engaged in small-scale agriculture and some commercial fishing. They had other income sources, so the reindeer industry was a much more commercialized enterprise from their point of view.

Political and economic power in the Muddusjärvi association was held mainly by the non-Skolts, although the Sevettijärvi men had come to exert some influence in herding matters because they participated so actively in the actual work. This was particularly true with respect to the "north herd" which was gathered and tended primarily by Skolts. After many years of complaints, the Skolts had finally prevailed on the association to build a second major roundup site at Silisjoki, north of Sevettijärvi, in order to facilitate the processing of the reindeer that tended to make their home in the northeastern part of the Muddusjärvi area. Nonetheless, the preponderance of decision-making power in the association continued in the hands of the westerners, and the chairman of the association was always elected from that faction.

The snowmobiles, which the westerners in the association obtained before the Skolts were able to afford them, conferred further competitive advantages on the association leaders. The Skolt reindeer men, who had already suffered some decline in herds during the beginning of the 1960s, were faced with a real crisis as the use of snowmobiles spread. Table 7 shows the dimensions of the deepening crisis.

In Table 7 the most significant item is the continuing loss in calves measured as a percentage of adult reindeer. The 1961–62 season had been bad, but it was nothing like the catastrophic "harvests" of 1966–67 and 1968–69, when calf production dropped to an average of about twelve percent (compared to the normal expectation of about thirty percent for Lapland as a whole).

Viewing the evidence concerning the decline of the Skolt Lapp herds during the middle of the 1960s, one is inclined to wonder where the animals went and who got them. Some of the reindeer were sold in order to make payments on snowmobiles, as was true for many other people in Lapland in that period. Also, rising living costs, including increased desires for consumer goods, led some of the Lapps to sell excessive numbers of animals.

However, the increased losses, especially in calves, were also clearly visible in the very large *increases* in *unidentified* animals. Many more of the calves that were brought to the roundup could not be claimed by their owners because they had been separated from their mothers during the drive to the corral, and the general loss of knowledge about the animals

Table 7.   Tallied Reindeer of the Skolt Lapps

Year[a]	Adult reindeer (includes animals sold and slaughtered)	Calves	%
1957–58	2230	700	31
1960–61	2678	?	?
1961–62	2167	480	22
1964–65	1829	436	24
1966–67	1338	187	14
1968–69	1498	151	10

[a] Only years for which these figures are available.

further reduced the possibilities of correct identification. Instead of a few tens of unmarked calves, there began to be hundreds of unidentified animals in the roundups. These animals were sold at auction, with the proceeds paid into the association treasury. The large increase in association income from this source was another unforeseen consequence of the snowmobile revolution and was a most timely "positive feedback" to the association. Without this windfall income, the organization would have been quickly bankrupted by the steeply rising costs of mechanized herding.

The rise in costs was especially clear in connection with the roundups, for at times there were a dozen or more snowmobilers out combing the backlands for reindeer, and each of them cost the association approximately $15.00 per day. Thus, each day of the on-again, off-again roundup in the winter of 1965 cost well over $100. (In 1965, the reindeer herders were still paid a set daily wage. The snowmobile drivers' compensation was supposed to cover their gasoline expenses and normal maintenance, with a modest additional increment for their "wages.")

In pre-snowmobile days the march from herding areas to the roundup location was usually accomplished by four or five herdsmen (traveling with reindeer sleds and skis), each of whom was paid about $3.00 per day. Thus, even very large herds of 6000 to 7000 reindeer cost the association only $12.00 to $15.00 per day for "delivery" to the corral. Of course, this rather efficient processing of reindeer at the roundup site was preceded by a considerable period of gathering and surveillance, sometimes for as long as two and one-half months. If the snowmobile herdsmen had worked with the reindeer for comparable periods of time, the costs would have been astronomical. Instead, the collecting of the animals had to be carried out as quickly as possible in order to keep costs down. As it is, the cost of association reindeer herding rose from about $1.30 per animal in 1963–64 to about $3.30 per animal in 1968–69. Thus, association fiscal policy added to the constellation of factors that decreased the amount of contact between herdsmen and their reindeer.

There is, however, another important feature of the auctioning of unmarked animals. The Muddusjärvi association leaders adopted the policy of auctioning reindeer in batches—twenty to thirty animals at a time. This practice was allegedly justified in terms of speed and convenience, but its main effect was to make it possible for individuals with wealth, or at least sources of credit, to buy up the lots of animals without having to bid against the small owners. This forced the Skolt Lapps (except for one or two families) almost totally out of the purchasing competition. Naturally, this situation was also disastrous for the less affluent westerners in the association as well.

The auctioning of unmarked animals at the end of each roundup session paraded the effects of the snowmobile herding before the eyes of the losers—the men whose herds were dwindling because they could not find and mark their yearly harvest of calves. To add insult to this ignominy, the small owners were effectively blocked from what had become for some herders a last-ditch herd maintenance strategy—*buying* reindeer calves to replace the ones that should have been out there in the herd with the adult females.

In 1969, following renewed appeals to higher levels of the Finnish government, the Skolts were at last granted an autonomous reindeer district. Map 8 shows the boundaries of the new

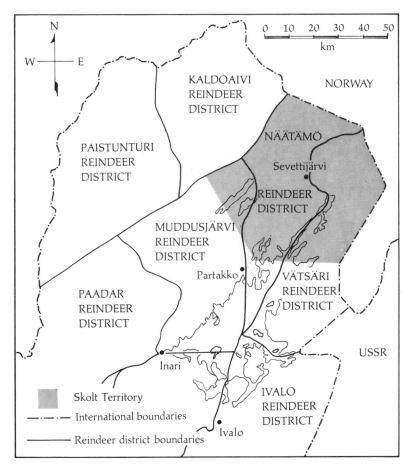

Map 8.   Reindeer association districts of northeastern Finnish Lapland, 1969.

association (named the Näätämö association) created from the northeastern half of the parent Muddusjärvi district. There are approximately thirty-six Skolt Lapp households in the newly created Näätämö district, as well as about ten to twelve families of other Lapps and Finns. Most of the non-Skolts are relatively uninvolved in reindeer activities.

Although the Skolts now have administrative control over their herding operations, conflicts with the westerners have continued concerning calf-marking, sale of unmarked animals, and other issues. In part the problems persist because there are no physical boundaries separating the two districts; while the men know that there are now two separate associations, the reindeer do not.

During the summer of 1971 the Muddusjärvi association men were carrying on a propaganda campaign intended to bring about a reuniting of the two districts. At the same time, they are seeking to bring pressure to bear against the possibility that a reindeer fence might be built between the two districts. The Skolts, on the other hand, now argue that they cannot gain full autonomy of herding operations until such a fence is built, totally separating their herds, both winter and summer, from those of the westerners. (Reindeer fences have become increasingly common in Lapland, as both herdsmen and national governments have sought to keep animals within national and local boundaries. In some areas conflicts between reindeer associations have been at least partially resolved by the wire-meshed barriers that prevent excessive interdistrict migrations of reindeer.)

There are some indications that the Skolts are faring somewhat better now that they have their own reindeer association. The reindeer and calf tallies for the first two years of autonomy were as follows:

Year	Adult reindeer (including those sold and slaughtered)	Calves	%
1969–70	1604	315	19
1970–71	1689	310	18

These figures appear to show some improvement over the previous year (1968–69), in which the Skolts got only 151 calves (a disastrous ten percent of total reindeer tally). It is, however, hard to tell at this juncture whether the statistics reflect "real" improvement or simply chance fluctuations in what Lapps sometimes refer to as "reindeer luck." In any case, for those

Skolt reindeer herders who have been able to stay in herding during this period, the fact that they can now make their own decisions about reindeer herding operations gives some sense of renewed hope and enthusiasm.

Considering the apparently disastrous consequences brought to them by snowmobile herding, we might expect that the Skolts would now seek to restore herding operations to something approximating pre-snowmobile practices. Such is not the case, however. The men are deeply divided on the issue of snowmobile use, since *some* of the members have apparently gained from the new situation. Also, the roster of active reindeer herders has changed considerably during the past ten years, particularly because of an influx of young men, most of whom are "pro-snowmobile" in orientation. The new autonomy in reindeer herding has not solved all of the Skolts' problems. Some of the social changes that have complicated the herding situation will be taken up in the next chapter.

Skolts and Snowmobiles in Vätsäri Association

As noted earlier, twelve Skolt Lapp families are in the Vätsäri reindeer district. These people were not affected by the formation of the new Näätämö association, for they have preferred to remain in the district in which they have gained a strong decision-making position. It is of great importance for our understanding of the snowmobile revolution to note that the economic and social impact of the machines has been quite different in the Vätsäri association. The technological change has apparently *not* resulted in a serious decline in their reindeer herds, although they have had to grapple with some serious organizational problems. The importance of both physical and social environment in shaping the outcomes of technological innovation is evident from the following:

1. The rocky and forested terrain in the Vätsäri district forced the herdsmen to be much more cautious and skeptical of mechanized herding than their neighbors in the Muddusjärvi area. Hence, they began herding with machines much later. Even in 1966–67 their herdsmen operated mainly on skis when collecting and transporting reindeer.

2. When snowmobiles came into greater use in the Vätsäri district it was not a situation forced on the Skolts by
other groups in the association, since the Skolts have in
recent years attained a position of approximate parity
with the non-Skolts in economic flexibility and decision-
making power within the association. An important factor
in this situation is the fact that the Skolts and non-Skolts
in the Vätsäri association are in quite similar ecological
positions in terms of subsistence activities and relationships to the marketing of reindeer.

The effects of environmental factors on the snowmobile revolution are further illustrated by the apparent successes of the Kaldoaivi herdsmen, to the north of the
Näätämö-Vätsäri area. In the wide-open tundra areas of
Kaldoaivi, the snowmobiles have great maneuvering advantage over the reindeer, so the deterioration of control
over the animals has not been nearly as drastic. Although
they have given up winter herds as well as many other
features of the pre-snowmobile annual cycle, the Kaldoaivi herdsmen have apparently had little difficulty in
processing their animals at their roundup enclosures.
Also, their calf-marking patterns were based on summer
roundups long before the advent of the machines, so they
have experienced very little reduction of efficiency in
identification and marking of calves for their proper owners.

Cash Costs of Reindeer Herding

The high costs of snowmobiles and their maintenance
have added a very large new monetary factor into the balance
sheet of reindeer herding, but the associations (including the
Näätämo association) have conveniently met these increased
costs by selling unmarked reindeer. For the individual herdsmen, however, there has been no windfall income from the sale
of unmarked animals. We must keep in mind that herding for
the association was only one aspect of reindeer activity for the
owners of the reindeer. Thus, the cost accounting of snowmobile use presents an entirely different picture when we examine
it from the point of view of the individual reindeer entrepreneur. The new high cost of operation accounts for many of

Table 8.   Estimate of Cash Costs of Participation in Herding
for One Year

Gasoline and other minor expenses	1000 Finnmarks
Normal repairs	200
Extra wear and tear (depreciation) of the snowmobile beyond that of normal usage	500
Total	1700
	($425)

the dropouts from mechanized herding, and has contributed to a number of other developments in the region, some of which will be reviewed in the next chapter.

Until the advent of the snowmobile, the cash cost of participating in herding activities was negligible. To be an active herder today requires a considerable reserve of cash, over and above the initial cost of purchasing a vehicle. Table 8 presents an estimate of the annual cost of snowmobile-borne participation in reindeer-herding activities.

In a study of snowmobilized reindeer herding in the Kaldoaivi district, north of Sevettijärvi, researchers have calculated that payments to the association herdsmen do not cover actual operating costs; so these herders are "subsidizing" the work of the association from their own assets (Müller-Wille and Aikio 1972). It should be noted, however, that participation in association herding activities is generally thought to improve the herdsman's chances of getting his "fair share" of calves. Thus, even those snowmobilers who are aware of their true cost of operation would usually consider the investment justified, *if they have a fairly sizeable number of reindeer.*

Of course, the modern reindeer herder must have a reliable snowmobile, which involves a purchase of about $1000 (U.S. dollars). The main point to be made here, however, is that the herdsman will, at best, recover his expenses by the end of the season; yet he must have some cash flexibility in order to participate fully in the system.

On the other hand, some herding activity is still carried out by ski-men in the Näätämö district. We note from Table 9 that in 1968–69, ski-men were significantly involved in several roundups, and a number of individuals participated only as ski-men, even though they owned machines. There is a continuing debate over the relative efficacy of snowmobiles compared to ski-men for rounding up animals. Clearly, certain portions of the Näätämö district are totally unsuited to snowmobile herding. However, it is important to point out that ski-men participate only in some roundups (in the heavily forested areas), and they usually must turn over the herds to the snowmobile men when they have completed their initial collecting work. The general feeling is that ski-men have much less prestige than snowmobile men, that they must work much harder, and their pay is less. Reindeer men should be fully mobile and able to participate in all aspects of herding, so that the restricted usefulness of ski-men appears to place them in a dependent, part-time role that is quite unsatisfactory from both psychological and economic points of view.

Table 9.   Man-Days in Näätämö Association Reindeer Work, 1968–69

	Snowmobile man-days	Ski man-days	Total adult reindeer processed
First roundup (end of Nov.)	30	14	318
Second roundup (Dec. 12)	24	11	316
Third roundup (Dec. 20)	20	8	274
Fourth roundup (Feb. 18)	21	22	153
Fifth roundup (Feb. 22)	21	2	205
	116	57	1266

Total participating herdsmen: 17

Photo 6.   Although ski-men still carry out some herding activity, their importance and prestige in the roundups is much diminished. *(author)*

Snowmobiles are now considered a household necessity in northeastern Lapland, and all except twelve of the households in the Sevettijärvi area have machines as of 1971. Most of these machines, however, are no longer employed extensively in reindeer herding since many households have effectively "dropped out" of reindeer husbandry. Many people simply cannot afford the added costs involved in herding activity. Their holdings of reindeer are now so small that the costs of participation far outweigh any possible gains. Their contact with the animals is limited to occasional attendance at round-ups.

Before the coming of mechanized herding a great deal of reindeer activity was carried out in the home herds. Also, every household had draught reindeer near home that required tending. Thus, even the families with only twenty to thirty animals spent time with their animals, castrating the young bulls, selecting animals for slaughter, and tending the females during calving season. (In Suenjel days the calving activities often included the whole family.)

From the point of view of some modern economists, the herding situation in the 1950s probably involved a certain amount of "disguised unemployment," since the adult males in many households often had a fair amount of leisure time between the various reindeer activities and other productive work. Nonetheless, the Skolts did not consider themselves to be unemployed in the wintertime. There were always some tasks waiting to be done, and most households did not see themselves as pressed for cash.

Now, however, the picture is radically altered. Since there are no winter herds, no draught reindeer, and no spring calving, the majority of able-bodied Skolt males cannot consider themselves to be reindeer herders in even a residual sense. They are now technologically unemployed. The fact of unemployment is made painfully clear by the fact that they now have *payments to meet*—monthly charges on their snowmobiles. Furthermore, they cannot even travel with their machines or engage in productive activities with them, unless they have money for gasoline. (One of the storekeepers told us of increased tensions developing between himself and the snowmobilers who seek gasoline on credit.) Many of the machines stand idle for periods of time because of lack of money for gasoline and needed repairs. Of course, the machine owners can always get from one place to another on their skis—but that's a humiliating comedown from the pleasant briskness of mechanized travel. And the trusty old geldings are not available to fill in for the snowmobiles in wood-hauling and other household tasks. In the period from 1967 on, more and more Skolt Lapps were registering as unemployed with the Finnish national employment service.

The introduction of a new gasoline-driven transportation system into northeastern Lapland brought with it some great advantages in speed and hauling capacity, but the costs in machines, fuel, and repairs are very high. The way in which the costs (and other problems) are managed and distributed varies from one social setting to another depending on the structures of economic exchange and political decision-making within the affected populations. In reindeer herding in Lapland the impact of the high costs has taken particular forms because of the structures of the reindeer associations that control major aspects of the economy. Reindeer herding is a highly individualized "free private enterprise" system, and the associations are usually dominated by individuals and families with the most social, economic, and political power. Therefore, there is the strong likelihood that the people in the weakest economic position will suffer losses because of their inability to compete, while some of the economically stronger families and groups may gain new advantages because of the mechanized transportation system. The results will be a restructuring of the social system.

CHAPTER NINE

The Social Impact
of the Snowmobile:
Differentiation and Stratification

The results of the snowmobile revolution—the mechanization of herding, the increased costs of participation, the decimation of the herds, and the great increase in the speed of winter transportation—have all had very far-reaching effects on the lifeways of Sevettijärvi people. I will turn now to an examination of some of the changes in social organization and related characteristics of the Skolt Lapps that can be linked to this technological change. The data suggest the following:

1. The cash cost of effective participation in herding is beyond the resources of some families, so that they have had to drop out of serious participation in herding activities.

2. The use of snowmobiles drastically changed the role requirements of reindeer herding. These changes, in general, favor youth over age, so that older herders (who would be the persons most likely to wish to continue in that economic activity) are being forced out in favor of younger men.

3. The almost total loss of individual and family control of the reindeer has made it extremely difficult and unrewarding for small owners to stay in reindeer herding.

4. Aside from the individual differences of involvement in herding, the coming of the snowmobile has pushed the entire Skolt Lapp population sharply in the direction of cash dependency and debt.

5. The increased dependence on cash has forced many individuals to seek new types of employment, with the result that there is now greater diversity of occupations than had been the case ten years ago, as well as greatly increased out-migration. (Of course, the availability of nonreindeer-connected jobs in the area is not a direct result of the snowmobile.)

6. In the shift to cash income and regular employment, as well as in the readjustment to the changed reindeer industry, some persons have achieved considerable success, while others have tended to fall out of the contest. *A general increase in socioeconomic inequalities has resulted.*

7. The increased speed with which people can get from one place to another has increased the rate of social interaction, drastically reduced the amount of time required for some important activities (for example, freight hauling), and has brought about changes in the scheduling and patterning of many group activities (for example, men return home from a roundup each night rather than camping out for many days at a time).

Changes in Role Requirements

By "role requirements" I mean the skills and characteristics (including motivation) that individuals must have in order to participate successfully in particular tasks, occupations, or other defined positions in the social system. For example, we usually assume that the role requirements for football players include a certain minimum of physical strength and hardiness; elementary schoolteachers should have skills in establishing positive relationships with children (among other important attributes); and political leaders should have decision-making capabilities. Most individuals occupying particular occupational roles are deficient in one or more of the needed skills or capabilities but manage nonetheless to perform their jobs sufficiently well because they have *most* of the requisite talents. Generally, the persons with the greatest skills (and resources) in the significant role requirements are the most successful in reaping the rewards (the profits, benefits, public acclaim) of particular social roles.

The following is a list of some of the principal requirements or skills in reindeer herding which *have been eliminated or drastically modified* by the snowmobile. Many of these activities were foci of conversation among reindeer men in 1958–59, as they compared experiences and indirectly assessed one another's performances and prestige.

1. Training, managing, and driving with draught reindeer.
2. Constructing harnesses and other equipment for draught reindeer use.
3. Lassoing reindeer in open country.
4. Recognizing individual reindeer (owner's marks, etc.) in open country.
5. All-day skiing in pursuit of straying reindeer.
6. Camping and "housekeeping" in forest and tundra.
7. Managing cows and calves during spring calving.
8. Controlled transporting of small herds of reindeer (for example, from roundup sites to home grazing grounds).
9. Training and managing herd dogs.

In place of these skills, the mechanized herdsman of the 1960s and 1970s must have:

1. Skills in maneuvering snow vehicles on rough terrain.
2. Ability to coordinate herding movements with other snowmobile drivers through visual cues (since voice communications do not carry over sound of motor).
3. Skills and resources (including money) for maintaining effective operation of motor vehicles.
4. Shrewd judgment concerning selling animals as they appear almost randomly in the various roundups.
5. Endurance and mobility required for attendance and participation *on relatively short notice* in different roundups at various locations throughout the year.

Comparing these two lists, one of the features we should note is that expertise in many of the skills that were important in the past was acquired through long years of experience, so that older herders were, in several respects, more competent than younger ones. Although physical endurance was important, many of the role enactments of reindeer herding were based on accumulated information, patience, and good judgment. In 1958–59 only one man in the community was definitely too old to participate actively in reindeer herding because of declining physical strength. He was seventy-one years old. Most of the other men of advanced years, including several in the sixty to sixty-five bracket, participated in many aspects of the work.

As the use of snowmobiles spread, the younger men were usually the more enthusiastic proponents of the machines, and they were the first to develop the skills for operating the machines in the backlands. Some of the more active young snowmobile herdsmen had never acquired the skills necessary for managing draught animals and other aspects of the pre-snowmobile herder's role; some of them were semidropouts until the machines made it possible for them to compete successfully in herding operations. Apparently the younger men were more willing to take physical and financial risks, and they were less concerned with the maintenance of the older herding regimen; also, may of them had had more experience with machinery as well as more exposure to new technical concepts as a result of both schooling and occasional wage-work activities. Their exposure to technical machinery during military training may have played a part in their readiness to work with the snowmobiles. In any case, they were quite successful in developing the new machine skills. We should also remind ourselves that the younger men had, for the most part, never experienced the intensive, "personalized" herding techniques that had characterized Skolt Lapp husbandry in prewar days. They therefore had less reason to put strong emphasis on intensive contacts between animals and men in the herding situation.

The slowness of the older men to develop proficiency with snowmobiles was almost certainly due to their attitudes toward reindeer herding rather than to a lack of mechanical capabilities as such. The prospect of eliminating many of the old herding practices was distasteful to many of the men who had been most active and successful in pre-snowmobile days.

Whatever the causes, there has been a distinct shift toward a younger age group in reindeer operations, and this shift would not have come about if there had been no change to mechanized herding.

Dropping out of Reindeer Herding

In 1960 a large percentage of the Skolt household heads were actively engaged in herding. Even those household heads who took no part in the official association work carried out a variety of tasks with their own family herds, especially during the latter part of the winter. In addition to the heads of families, some young men in their teens and early twenties also were involved with reindeer work. There were, in fact, very few other activities or occupations available to them.

Table 10 gives a breakdown by age categories of active reindeer herders of the Sevettijärvi area for 1960 and 1971.

The column labeled "Projected 1971" shows my estimate of the herding participation that would have been maintained if large-scale changes had not occurred in the system. It is based on the general assumption that active reindeer herdsmen maintain their participation in the system as long as health permits. Even serious losses of reindeer would not ordinarily cause a man to quit herding—provided such losses came about within the normal course of variations of "herding luck." Of the herdsmen active in 1960, only two or three have dropped out because of possibly attractive alternative sources of income. Some of the older men would have dropped out because of poor health and a few younger men not active in 1960 would have joined the ranks of association herdsmen. (Three herdsmen died during this decade.) The total number of herdsmen should have increased slightly.

The actual age profile of reindeer herders is quite different from this projection, however. We note in Table 10 that many of the men who were in the thirty-one to fifty age bracket in 1960 (and would be in their forties and fifties in 1971) have

Table 10. Age of Active Reindeer Herders, 1960 and 1971

Age of active reindeer herders[a]	1960	Projected 1971	Actual 1971[b]
15–20	4	4	7
21–30	13	8	10
31–40	7	12	13
41–50	12	6	2
51–60	4	10	2
61+	1	3	3
Totals	41	43	37

[a]"Active" herders are those who participate in association work *in addition to* tending their own animals.

[b]Includes "part-time" herders.

dropped out of active participation. Their place has been taken by the younger men. The trend is also clear if we compare the number of *household heads* active in 1960 and in 1971. In spite of a small increase in the total number of households because of marriages contracted during the period (from forty-eight in 1960 to fifty-six in 1971), the number of household heads active in reindeer herding declined from twenty-five to nineteen. About a dozen men who were heads of households engaged in reindeer herding in 1960 have simply dropped out of the action because of the advent of snowmobiles.

These figures do not actually reflect the full extent of the decline in numbers of herders. As described earlier, before the snowmobile much of the reindeer-herding cycle was concerned with the care and maintenance of home herds. Some herders took relatively little part in association action, yet spent a great deal of time with their own animals, especially in the latter part of the winter. These men are not included in the list of "active reindeer herders" for 1960; yet their principal economic pursuits were basically aimed at reindeer husbandry. These "home herdsmen" now have *no* herds. Some of them have lost *all* their animals, but even those who still have a few head take no part in herding activities except for attending roundups occasionally.

Some of the older men who have "retired" from reindeer herding were pushed out because of physical or social complications in their herding effectiveness. Here are some samples.

Feodor Osipoff[1] was forty-six years old in 1960, and at that time had one of the largest herds in the Näätämö area. He was regarded as an effective herder in most respects, particularly in active operations in the backlands. However, at reindeer roundups he was thought to drink too heavily on occasion, and therefore he did not always maintain good control over the sales of animals and other transactions in the important festive atmosphere of the roundup enclosures.

In the early 1960s his herds began to decline. He did not buy a snowmobile during the first crucial years of the technological transition. Indeed, he did not have the cash for a snowmobile, probably in part because of occasional heavy expenditures on beer and other alcoholic drinks. By 1965–66 he no longer took part in herding operations, as most of the active herdsmen operated with snowmobiles. By 1971 his herd had dwindled from a pre-snowmobile high of nearly 200 to a mere seventeen reindeer.

Because of his growing needs for cash (including the expenses of the second-hand snowmobile purchased in 1969), Feodor signed up in the unemployment register of the Finnish employment service and has been working at various locations in Inari commune on road crews during recent winters. His sons have not continued in reindeer herding.

Maxim, who is Feodor's brother, was also an active herdsman in 1960, with a herd that numbered about seventy head in 1958. With a large and growing family, he apparently could not easily afford to buy a snowmobile during the mid-1960s, and in any case he was against the conversion to mechanized herding. He tried to maintain his string of draught reindeer until 1968 but finally had to give up. Even the draught reindeer could not be maintained effectively under the altered herding structure.

In addition to his opposition to snowmobiles, he was increasingly bothered by some health problems that hampered his effectiveness. Maxim's herd is down to thirteen reindeer, according to the official figures of 1971.

---

[1]This and the following names are pseudonyms.

Boris Kotala is a member of the Vätsäri association and was an active herder in 1960, although he was already nearly sixty years old. Since the mechanization of herding in the Vätsäri district was slow in developing, one cannot say that he was forced out of herding by the advent of the machines. However, his son Eero had become an active herder by 1967 and had already purchased a snowmobile in the fall of 1966. Since then, Eero has been quite successful in building up the family herd and is reputed to be one of the most effective young men in the local association. Thus, Boris has been able to retire gracefully from reindeer herding because the family's interests are ably represented both at roundups and in herd-gathering operations.

A few of the dropouts from reindeer herding are younger men who were already effective herdsmen in the old system and were apparently doing very well in adjusting to mechanized herding when they made the decision to change their economic pursuits. For example:

Nikolai Asimoff was one of the very young but active herders of 1960. Since his father was fairly old and semiretired from reindeer herding, Nikolai was the primary representative of the family in herding activities. He bought his first snowmobile in 1966–67, when the first Moto-Skis appeared in the local area. He became one of the most active herdsmen in the new, mechanized system; and in 1968–69 he was the second most active herder in the Näätämö district, in terms of work days for the association.

Nonetheless, the following year he got word from one of his wife's relatives, who spoke of employment possibilities at a large Swedish factory. He has now been working in Sweden for three years and visits his kinsmen at Sevettijärvi during his summer vacations. The family still has a few head of reindeer, but except for obtaining an occasional animal for meat, the economic importance of their reindeer herding is minimal.

Mechanized herding attracted the interest of some younger men who were indifferent herders in pre-snowmobile days. The following is an example of a young man who was apparently becoming a successful mechanized herder when he made the decision to quit herding activity.

Evvan Andreev was a young man just back from military service in 1958–59 and seemed to be rather unskilled in reindeer herding, although his father showed great patience and care in grooming him for that occupation. The fact that the family had fairly sizeable herds (by local standards) certainly should have been an advantage in motivating him to improve his herding skills.

In the early 1960s he worked in logging camps somewhat more than he did in reindeer herding. With the advent of the snowmobile, the family was among the first Skolt Lapp households to acquire a machine. In fact, by 1966 their household owned two snowmobiles, while most families at that time still had none.

Evvan became active in reindeer herding. The old herdsman's skills that he had failed to acquire were now no obstacle, whereas his work with machinery in the logging camps aided in his adaptation to the new age of mechanization. For a few years he seemed to be successful at reindeer herding. Like some of the other more affluent herders, he and his brother (with their father's help) bought reindeer from the association in an attempt to build up their herds. Even though the family has had the advantages of early snowmobile ownership and sufficient economic resources to purchase more animals, they have reluctantly come to the conclusion that it is not economically advantageous to invest heavily in herding at the present time. Evvan has taken a full-time job in the government forest service, while his brother works full time for the government telephone-telegraph service. The aggregate family herd is still one of the three largest in the Näätämö association, but in spite of great personal efforts and monetary investment, even their herds have declined slightly.

Aside from the factor of age, the dropouts from reindeer herding can be divided into two main categories: "losers" and "adapters." Many of the men who have quit reindeer herding have done so because they effectively had no choice. They lost most of their reindeer, and they do not have the economic means to keep up snowmobile equipment and other aspects of involvement in reindeer-herding competition. On the other hand, Nikolai and Evvan, for example, seem to have had a clear choice, and they chose to leave reindeer herding because they perceived other alternatives to be more acceptable. Nikolai decided to take a chance on wage work in Sweden because of the promise of a steady income much greater than that possible from reindeer herding in the Näätämö region. Evvan also saw wage work opportunities as providing a better income for himself and family, although his employment is within the local area, thus involving fewer risks and sacrifices.

Men Who Stayed In

The men who have stayed in reindeer herding, at least on a part-time basis, are as varied in their adaptive responses as those who dropped out.

The Osipoff brothers, Sergei and Iutsa, are examples of men who have remained active in reindeer work all through the snowmobile transition, but with mixed success. In the old Suenjel days when their father was alive, the Osipoffs had more reindeer than any other family in the community. In fact, the ancestors of the Osipoffs may have been the originators of expanded reindeer herding in Suenjel in response to the sharp decline in wild reindeer during the early part of the nineteenth century.

During the period of rebuilding—in the 1950s—Sergei had managed to increase his herd to forty or fifty head, but he lagged well behind his brothers, especially Iutsa, who had about 130 animals in 1958–59. Both men had married after the war, and both had households totalling eight persons, of which there were as yet no sons old enough to participate in reindeer activities.

Sergei often talked of the successful reindeer herding methods of prewar days, and he was strongly insistent on the necessity for a separate Skolt Lapp association so that they could recover their former intensive control over the herds. Since Sergei was not as outgoing as his brothers, he did not participate directly in association herding as much as they did, preferring to spend a lot of time in his own home-herd activities. This arrangement may have reflected a division of responsibilities among the Osipoff brothers, for they cooperated quite closely in maintaining their joint winter herd.

From Sergei's point of view the herding situation had taken a turn for the worse in the early 1960s, and the advent of the snowmobile simply pushed them over the brink. He suffered rapid losses in both adult reindeer and calves, and he was insistent that the snowmobiles were ruining the reindeer herds completely. He did not want to participate in the mechanized

herding, although he continued to operate as a ski-man during
the periods when the conflicts and invidious comparisons between the ski-men and the snowmobile men were becoming
increasingly painful.

In 1966–67, Sergei's oldest son acquired a used Evinrude
machine and began to take part in some herding activities. The
choice of the Evinrude as the family machine indicates that both
Sergei and his son saw their primary transportation needs to be
in household freight trips, wood hauling, and general travel. (By
1966–67, it was well known that the heavier machines were not
suitable for intensive reindeer-herding action.)

In 1970–71, Sergei's total herd was tallied at just seven adult
reindeer. He was, for all practical purposes, finished, and the
family had to buy reindeer meat for household consumption.
His son had signed up for unemployment and had been admit-
ted to a carpentry course in Rovaniemi, from which he hoped
to develop steady employment, although it might require that
he live in the population centers of south Lapland.

Sergei's adaptation to the near-elimination of his stake in
herding is probably a reflection of his deep identification with
the reindeer industry. Although he has virtually no reindeer of
his own, he continues to work for the association as a ski-man
and, with the help of two of his sons, he has built coffee houses
at two of the Näätämö roundup sites. Thus, he has tried to turn
his continuing attendance at the roundups into a small source
of income. Also, his boys haul meat for meat buyers and engage
in other odd jobs, using the new Swedish Sno-trik that Sergei
bought. In addition to the economic contributions of his three
sons, Sergei's household economy also receives some help from
daughter Anni's work. She has had occasional employment as
a domestic servant in Kaamanen and was working on a farm in
Norway during the summer of 1971.

Sergei has evidently been extremely careful with his very
slender economic resources, for the household ranks well in the
top half of households in terms of their material style of life.
They have a telephone, snowmobile, and chain saw, in addition
to which they have taken out government loans to expand their
log cabin into a four-room frame structure. In addition to a
long-term loan and a grant from the government, this expansion
will cost Sergei about 4000 Finnmarks from his own pocket.

A hundred yards farther down the lakeshore, brother Iutsa's house was undergoing a similar expansion during the summer of 1971. From outward appearances, at least, he should be
able to afford this expenditure somewhat more easily than Ser-

gei, since he still has sufficient reindeer to provide a significant addition to his household economy. During the early part of the 1960s he was among the most active Skolt Lapp herdsmen in the Muddusjärvi association, and he was relatively quick to try his hand at mechanized herding.

Iutsa bought a Swedish Ockelbo in the winter of 1965–66 but found that the machine had serious design deficiencies for reindeer herding. The fact that he had more reindeer than most of his neighbors probably accounts for Iutsa's ability to invest in the machines at a fairly early date, since he was able to sell more reindeer for cash. His household economy is also given an important boost through his mother's old age pension, which amounted to something close to $80.00 a month in 1970.

Iutsa was one of several Skolts who bought the new Swedish Moto-Ski in 1966–67. He found this machine to be quite effective in herding, and he got a lot of service from it before he traded it in on a Sno-trik in 1969. In 1970 he again traded in his machine, thus maintaining his policy of frequent trade-ins as a way of minimizing out-of-pocket maintenance costs.

By 1970–71 Iutsa, like his brother, had a daughter working on a farm in Norway and two sons who were old enough for reindeer work and could make other contributions to the family economy. The official reindeer tally of 1970–71 listed Iutsa with forty adult animals and fifteen calves. Thus, Iutsa is still very much in competition to stay in the reindeer business, and the fact that his herd included fifteen calves in 1971 looks very good indeed. This represents a calf production of nearly forty percent —a rate that could result in a rapid rebuilding of his herd if it can be maintained.

One of the other Osipoff brothers died in the early 1960s; the fourth member of this once-powerful group is quite ill and has lost all his reindeer. Their cousins, who also had respectable herds in 1958–59, have suffered serious declines; although Demian Osipoff, with thirty-six head and nineteen calves, also seems to be making a comeback.

The younger men who have come into reindeer herding within the past few years represent two different types of households. On the one hand, several of them are sons of the most active older generation of herders. For example, there are five younger Osipoffs among the newer herdsmen. The other type of situation that has also produced a number of the younger herdsmen is a set of households that lacked able-bodied male protagonists for a long time. Thus, several of the new young herders are the sons of widows, or of crippled, nonherding fathers.

Aleksi Prokoff, for example, was just a young boy when his father died in 1958. His mother had always been active in all aspects of herding, however; and she continued to look after the family herds, working closely with her brother, whose house is only seventy-five meters away—practically in the same yard. The young Aleksi grew up in a household in which reindeer herding was particularly highly valued, and both mother and uncle provided role models and practical instruction.

The Prokoffs are in the Vätsäri district—in which the Skolts have fared somewhat better than their kinsmen in the Näätämö district; the young boys growing up in that area have not been faced with the degree of deterioration in morale that is so pervasive among their Näätämö neighbors.

There is only one Skolt Lapp family in the Näätämö association that can be regarded as really successful in the new herding situation. The Sergeev family's reindeer now constitute about thirty percent of the total association holdings. The two brothers, Peatt and Kiurel, are both very active herders; in fact, Kiurel was the single most active herdsman in the 1968–69 season (in terms of man-days of work) and Peatt was the herding foreman for the north end of the Muddusjärvi district. (At that time, the split between Muddusjärvi and Näätämö was not yet final, but the Skolt herders had been given partial autonomy in the organization of work.)

Kiurel was already a full-time herder in the late 1950s. Peatt was employed in wage labor until 1959–60, when he decided to become a herdsman. Since both brothers have had considerable experience in wage work, they have acquired economic means and skills with machines. Also, the fact that Kiurel is a bachelor and Peatt did not marry until the end of the 1960s placed them in advantageous positions with regard to personal mobility and financial flexibility.

It is interesting to note that Peatt's and Kiurel's father, who is still physically active, has never been much interested in reindeer herding. His special adaptation to local ecological possibilities has been to concentrate on lake fishing, leaving the care of family herds to his sons. On the other hand, his brothers were dedicated herdsmen; apparently they served as important role models for Peatt and Kiurel.

Although the Sergeev brothers did not invest in snowmobiles until the winter of 1966–67, they have expanded their "fleet" to the point where the family now owns four machines, one of which is driven by the father. Peatt owns two machines, one of which is regularly used by his nephew Andrei, who is regarded as his "right-hand man" in reindeer-herding activities.

Peatt and Kiurel have greatly increased their holdings by purchasing unidentified reindeer at the Muddusjärvi and Näätämö roundups. One or the other—often both men—have been present at practically all significant reindeer action around the district during the past several years, and they are frequently the directors of herding operations. In association meetings they are more vocal and outspoken than most of the rest of the membership and see themselves as formulators of policy.

The Sergeev brothers are probably the strongest local partisans of snowmobilized reindeer herding. From their point of view, the use of ski-men has entirely failed to produce results, and the improvement of herding in the district must depend on improved techniques of snowmobile use. This point of view is in opposition to the views expressed by many other persons in the association, who insist that snowmobile herding will not succeed in the rougher, forested part of the district. Many of the criticisms that have been made of the snowmobiles, Peatt notes, are criticisms of improper or careless handling and tactics. He argues that effective snowmobile herding is an art that many of the local people have not yet learned. But their mistakes of the past should not be used to deny the utility of the machines.

Figure 9 summarizes the shift in patterns of herding participation from 1960 to 1971. Of the forty-one Skolt herdsmen who were active in 1960, eight have died or retired for reasons of health; nineteen have dropped out of reindeer activities to take up wage-labor positions or other occupations; and only fourteen continue as active herdsmen. Most of the herding is now carried out by younger men, many of whom were too young to be reindeer herders in 1960. Twenty-three persons are now active, at least on a part-time basis, who were not involved in association herding in 1960.

If the snowmobile had been the only important new factor affecting the lives of the Skolt Lapps, my review of "dropouts" versus "stay-ins" in reindeer herding would provide us with a set of cases from which we could assess the chief causes of socioeconomic "successes" and "failures." However, modernization processes in northern Finnish Lapland have introduced a number of alternative economic opportunities for the

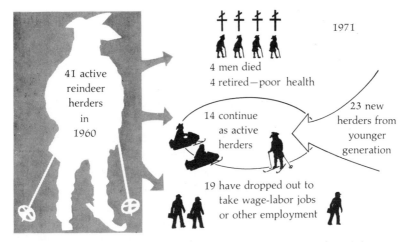

Figure 9.   Only one third of the active Skolt herders in 1960 were still participating in reindeer operations in 1971. Nearly half dropped out to pursue other economic activities.

Skolt Lapps and their neighbors; so it is not possible to equate dropping out of reindeer herding with economic failure. Some of the cases described above (for example, Nikolai Asimoff and Evvan Andreev) illustrate the fact that a few of the men who have quit reindeer herding are among the more economically successful individuals. Assessment of "successful adaptation" must therefore include much more than reindeer herding.

New Patterns of Out-Migration

One of the new alternatives that some of the men have adopted is that of temporary or even permanent migration to other employment areas. The direct connection between events in reindeer herding and these recent increases in out-migration is evident when we contrast the Skolt males with their female counterparts. As described in Chapter Two, the Skolt girls have been eager to leave the Sevettijärvi area, either through marriage or through finding domestic work or other unskilled employment in the population centers. This pattern of female out-migration was already well established in the early 1950s.

Among the men, on the other hand, there was practically no out-migration until the middle and late 1960s. Their new search for wage employment outside the local area was brought about by several converging factors.

1. The snowmobile (and other newly available commercial goods) created very greatly increased needs for cash.

2. The advent of mechanized herding had created a situation of "technological unemployment" for the men who were forced out of full-time herding activities.

3. New policies of the Finnish employment service also had a strong influence on out-migration. The government has begun to pay unemployment compensation and has made increased efforts to find work for unemployed persons, particularly in road crews that are building and maintaining Finland's rapidly expanding network of paved roads.

4. The newest development in the Finnish employment service is the provision for schooling in various employable skills. Unemployed persons are given room and board, plus a small daily cash allowance, while they attend these courses. Skolt Lapps have attended training programs in automobile undercoating, manufacturing tourist souvenirs, windshield repair and replacement, carpentry and construction, assembly-line machine work, and others. This new program of the Finnish employment service will have a major impact on Lappish labor migration; however, it is important to note that the Skolts would probably have been much slower to participate in this program if the effects of the snowmobile had not pushed them out of their established winter activities.

5. The completion of the road to Sevettijärvi (1967), together with a very large increase in tourism all over Lapland, has led to contacts between the Skolts and persons in the south who are in positions to influence and aid in job placement. For example, several young Skolts are now in the industrial city of Tampere because of the efforts of one Finnish entrepreneur who befriended some of the local people during his vacation trips into the area.

In spite of the recent increases in male out-migration, a large imbalance between males and females still persists. Table

Table 11.   Out-Migration of Sevettijärvi Skolts

	Permanently emigrated	Stayed in community	Total
Sons	28	58	86
Daughters	45	33	79

Note: These figures include sons and daughters of the original fifty households that settled in Sevettijärvi in 1949. They are approximately correct, although some of the daughters who emigrated in the early 1950s may have been "forgotten" in this tabulation. Exact figures fluctuate somewhat as unmarried persons, especially sons, return home for indefinite periods.

11 presents these out-migration data. Robert Paine has documented similar sex imbalances for a coastal Lapp community in Norway (Paine 1965).

Incipient Social Stratification

When the snowmobile was first introduced into northeastern Lapland in 1961–63, the first Skolt Lapps to acquire them were individuals who were more socioeconomically successful than their fellows in the ways I have just suggested. In terms of ownership of material goods and participation in a number of different cash-earning activities, the first snowmobile owners were mainly from the upper quartile of the Skolt Lapp community (Pelto, *et al.,* 1968). This is, of course, to be expected, given the high cost of snowmobiles. The important fact, however, is that the acquisition of snowmobiles conferred additional adaptive advantages on those families who were already becoming socioeconomic leaders.

The snowmobile has had the effect of introducing a large element of "starting capital" into the economy such that some persons who may have the skills necessary for effective reindeer herding and other activities are unable to compete in these pursuits because they do not have the economic means to get started. Now, the difference that has come about is clearly a matter of degree, but the effect seems to be rather evident. Differentiation of the more successful families from those that are at the bottom of the economic hierarchy is, to a rapidly increasing degree, associated with the possession of costly technological devices and *cash reserves*. Economic competition in the region is structured more and more in terms of competing technological inventories rather than basic physical skills and wisdom. As the differentiation among the families increases, the competitive chances of the children in the poorer families are reduced, at least as far as participation in the reindeer-herding industry is concerned.

Table 12 shows the developing stratification of economic means among the fifty-one Skolt Lapp households. (I am including the Skolts from the Vätsäri association in these figures.) The same *general* economic forces are operating on them, even though they have not had to experience quite the degree of reindeer-herding disaster. Several points stand out in these illustrations. The "Material Style of Life" index which is explained more fully in Appendix C, shows that there is a rapidly growing differentiation in the household furnishings and technical goods available to the different households.

The index contains two different kinds of items: washing machines, gas lights, and oil heaters are "conveniences" which presumably add to the comfort and feeling of well-being in these families, but they are not "capital goods" in the sense of items that markedly improve the adaptive capacity of the household. The snowmobiles, chain saws, telephones, and automobiles, on the other hand, are technological features that are essential, or at least highly important, for improving an individual's physical mobility and speed of communication. Thus, people who are relatively high on the "Material Style of Life" scale are those families who have both "modern comforts" and technological aids for active socioeconomic competition.

When we look at the relationship between significant participation in reindeer herding and position on our index, we find that households that have maintained a degree of involvement in the traditional economy are mainly in the upper half of the techno-economic scale (see Appendix D). To a large

Table 12.   Scale of "Material Style of Life" among Skolt Lapps
and Their Neighbors

	Scale type[a]	Skolts	Other Lapps	Finns	Total
I	Household has all listed material items	1	0	1	2
II	All items except TV	2	1	1	4
III	All except TV and refrig.	3	0	0	3
IV	All except TV, refrig., and automobile.	2	0	0	2
V	See Appendix C for definitions of these types.	2	1	0	3
VI	See Appendix C for definitions of these types.	9	1	0	10
VII	See Appendix C for definitions of these types.	3	0	0	3
VIII	See Appendix C for definitions of these types.	8	1	2	11
IX	See Appendix C for definitions of these types.	15	3	5	23
X	See Appendix C for definitions of these types.	4	1	1	6
XI	Not even snow-mobile or chain saw.	2	1	0	3
	Total households				70

Note: Households with more than one nuclear family are considered single households in this list.

[a]See Appendix C for the full Guttman scale, including item list.

extent this reflects the fact that active involvement in reindeer herding is now predicated, or at least enhanced, by ownership of several of the items in the Material Style of Life index.

It is interesting to note that the people in the upper half of our scale of techno-economic success control the major share of both the reindeer herding *and* the wage labor opportunities within the local area. Of the total of approximately twenty to twenty-four regular cash-earning jobs in the area that are held by Skolt Lapps, all except two or three of them are controlled by people in the *upper half* of the Material Style of Life index. This is not surprising, of course, in the case of the older employment cases, since the incumbents of these would have been expected to purchase the items in the Material Style of Life index from money earned on the job. However, almost all of the *new* occupations that have opened up in the past two years have also been captured by those people who needed them least—the people who were already economic leaders in earlier years (cf., Pelto, *et al.,* 1968). Thus, everything new that takes place in the increasingly differentiated economic pattern appears to work to the advantage of the families that *already have* the predominance of economic power as expressed in control of local inventories of scarce resources.

Until about 1960 the principal economic activity available to Skolt Lapp males was in reindeer herding. There was a moderate amount of differentiation in herding success, and there was also some differentiation among families in fishing activities, summer wage work, and other secondary economic pursuits. The advent of the road during the middle 1960s was accompanied by increasing economic complexity, expanded household needs, and greatly escalated contacts between the Skolts and the "outside world." Even if the snowmobile had never come to Lapland, these factors certainly would have contributed to further economic differentiation among the Skolt families. Trends of this sort were apparent in 1962—in differences in food supplies, upkeep of homes, dress styles of teenagers, and other aspects of life-style.

The remarkable transformation in the reindeer-herding situation during the 1960s greatly increased the tempo of differentiation and intensified the contrasts between the families with means and those who were increasingly handicapped in economic competition. Fortunately, many of the families in the lower end of the Material Style of Life index receive some income from the increasingly bountiful Finnish system of social security. They receive veteran's benefits, old age pensions, invalid's payments, and other transfer funds. Therefore, the material deprivation in food and other necessities among these Lappish families is not as serious as that found among the poor in many parts of the United States. Their socioeconomic situation is not nearly as desperate as that of most American Indian families, for example.

The social effects of the differentiation process are not particularly evident at this time. Although the differences in equipment, household goods, and other possessions provide signals of differential economic status, people who have been living in relatively egalitarian terms do not immediately begin practicing social exclusiveness to match their economic differences. There are some indications that differences in educational aspirations may be developing, but other clear signs of social stratification behavior are not evident—yet.

The process of developing inequality brought about by the snowmobile is most apparent as a growing "techno-economic differentiation," rather than an overall socio-cultural stratification of life-styles and social intercourse.

Who Made It to "The Top"?

One of my main concerns in this study has been to trace the internal processes through which economic and social differentiation occurs. In pursuing this interest, one important question which needs to be raised is: What are the characteristics of the individuals who "succeed" as compared with those who are less "successful"? Since the achievements of the families high on the index of Material Style of Life are not due to clearly inherited differences in starting capital, nor to more generalized class advantage, how can we account for their present situation? An assessment of the causes of individual success or failure during the postwar period would require a full-scale study, much beyond the scope of this book. Some suggestions can be set out, however, which are no more than rough hypotheses for future research.

A Comment on "Economic Success and Failure"

I should make clear that I am using the terms "success" and "failure" in a very limited range of meaning. From my research among the Lapps and their neighbors I found rather strong evidence that the majority of them desire material items such as those listed in Appendix C, and they want to have sufficient money to buy these and other goods, in order to attain a certain standard of living. They also appear to value successful performance of occupational roles (reindeer herding and other work) which produce goods and money. In addition to the evidence concerning the attitudes and motivations of the Lapps, it appears that acquisition of various technical items is a fairly effective indicator of economic flexibility among these people.

Therefore, I am using the term "economic success" to refer specifically to the acquisition of material items and financial means as reflected in the Material Style of Life index. This is not meant to imply that persons who are high on this scale are of greater excellence in other aspects of life. They are not necessarily more psychologically stable, better sexually adjusted, or higher in "moral" standards. "Successful adaptation" in my discussion simply refers to capability in "making a living" in terms that conform to current views among the Lapps.

Some of the relatively unsuccessful cases are perhaps easiest to analyze first. Poor health seems very clearly involved in several instances of men who have remained economically marginal. Since physical ability has been so closely related to success in reindeer herding and other economic activities, several individuals with uncertain health are among the emerging category of "techno-economic marginality."

Excessive alcohol use also seems to be implicated, for at least five of the more notable "dropouts" from reindeer herding were characterized by at least occasional heavy drinking in situations that required sober and effective action. Nearly everyone in the Sevettijärvi region uses alcohol at times, but there is a fine line between controlled drinking and the overuse of alcohol that reduces economic efficiency. (There are only one or two persons in the community who may be "alcoholic" in the usual medical sense.) A contributing factor in this picture is the loss of economic flexibility that comes from the high cost of alcoholic drink. A few of the men may have experienced an interaction effect between nascent economic failure and increased alcohol consumption.

The problem of financial flexibility was particularly central in the early years of the snowmobile transition. Several of the unsuccessful cases were men with insufficient cash and reindeer reserves to purchase machines in the period of 1965–68. It appears that herders who managed to get machines during that period were able to stay in the economic competition; those who did not were effectively squeezed out of reindeer activities, as well as some other economic niches.

Geographic marginality may have contributed to differential techno-economic success, for a few of the least successful members of the community are located in places that are far from the main lines of information flow. It may be suggested, however, that some of these individuals may have chosen their locations in order to stay out of the centers of social interaction. Also, a few of them appear to have been somewhat indifferent to prospects of economic success or failure. Thus, it is possible that a small number of these socially marginal individuals are not in any full sense "techno-economic failures," since they are uninterested in striving for the newly available material opportunities.

Some isolated instances of relative techno-economic failure appear to involve the following factors: lack of able-bodied men in the family (for example, in the homes of some widows); apparent lack of mental and physical capability, either from genetic inheritance or early experience; and misfortunes, accidents, or other chance events.

The characteristic that stands out most clearly in the case of the techno-economically most successful persons are those of physical mobility, high activity levels, nonspecialization, and centrality in information flow.

The men who appeared to be most well adapted and successful in 1958–59 were persons who were able to travel widely in order to take part in a great variety of activities. They were the men who went to all the roundups in the region, were active in all phases of herding, and who were in attendance at various social events as well. From my field notes I find that these more active persons tended to be frequent visitors and also were hosts more often than other people. They tended to have more physical equipment (such as boat motors) that aided their mobility.

Mobility and activity go hand in hand. These more successful individuals appeared, on the whole, to build more boats and fishing camps; they planted more potatoes; and they engaged in other economic and social activities. It is not possible to identify the focus of their activities as either "traditional" or "progressive." It seems to me that these men have been more active in *all* sectors of the social and economic system. Arto Sverloff, for example, has been reindeer herder, herding foreman, taxi driver, freight and passenger hauler, postman, and (incidentally) anthropological research assistant. Another "successful adaptor" has been a full-time reindeer herder under both old and new systems, and has been herding foreman. On the other hand, he has been active in snowmobile racing and was the first Skolt householder in the region to complete the building of a new four-room frame house to replace the old government-built log cabin. The activities of another successful family have included active reindeer herding (including herd foreman duties), salmon fishing, guiding for tourists and travelers, operating the telephone exchange, full-time employment in logging for the forest service, and other participation in wage work.

Several of the most techno-economically active families of the area are located near the hub of communications—at the village center which includes stores, school, health center, and church. The village center is the mail distribution point, the telephone exchange is located there, and the rather extensive influence of the local school is felt most strongly in this cluster of households.

To a certain extent the locations of the various families in the Sevettijärvi area were chosen by the families themselves, although it is clear that not all families had a clear choice in selecting house sites. Whatever may have been the benefits of information flow that have accrued to more centrally located families, they could not have been predicted from the situation in the planning stages of the move to the new area. And, to a certain extent, "centrality" in the communications network has been created and modified by the social interactions of the families.

Some external environmental factors, therefore, have been influential in affecting differential techno-economic expansion. We must also keep in mind that the vagaries of accident, sickness, and just plain bad luck are to a considerable extent (although not wholly) outside the realm of individuals' adaptive acting and deciding. Some well-founded folklore of reindeer herding also emphasizes the role of "luck" in promoting growth of herds and general success with reindeer.

But a very considerable part of the adaptive successes, however modest, of some of the Skolt Lapps compared with others appears to derive from the personal characteristics of particular individuals. Without attempting the difficult task of finding the *"causes"* for these personal differences, my argument can be summarized with the following observations.

On the whole, the more successful Skolts during this difficult time of rapid modernization are characterized by a very considerable flexibility of personal behavior, a self-confidence in individual task performance, and a high level of personal initiative in the accomplishment of economic work. These people are what David McClelland (1961) has referred to as "moderate risk takers." On the whole, the personal behavioral style that is particularly evident in the more successful Skolts is that of "individualism," which I have described at length in an earlier work (Pelto 1962), following initial field research of 1958–59.

The characteristic individualism of the Skolts does not include any strong element of aggressive competition with other persons, although such competition is always present to some extent in fairly complex socioeconomic systems. Rather, individual Skolts have, at least in the past, focused on the struggle and "competition" between self and nonhuman environment instead of the complexities of social interaction and manipulation. In the past a man's adaptive success depended to a very great degree on his effective management of directly perceived information from and interaction with the reindeer, the physical terrain, and his personal equipment (sleds, harness, fishing gear, etc.).

Now the adaptive focus is shifting rapidly to much more

socially involved sectors of behavior, especially to relationships with wage labor employers as well as commercial operators and tourists. But *some* of the socially *un*involved personal
characteristics of these people have continued to be of adaptive
significance (for example, in maintenance and repair of machinery, especially when operating in the backlands with
snowmobiles). The more successful Skolt adaptors appear to
exhibit a flexible mixture of individualistic *and* more socially
involved personal style (cf., Pelto 1971).

Increased Social Interaction

Snowmobiles have contributed in many indirect ways to
increased social interdependence because of both technical and
economic aspects of the machines. Also, the greatly increased
speed of travel has added directly to the intensity of social
interaction. Each individual traveling about by snowmobile
can get around to more places in a shorter time. There are now
about three times as many reindeer roundups as in pre-snowmobile days; and while there may be a slight dropoff in attendance at some of the more marginal roundups, the overall
effect is a clear increase in the number of times that people
come together at the roundup sites. (Many people continue to
attend roundups quite regularly even though they do not participate in association herding and have very few reindeer of
their own.)

Another contribution to social interaction comes from the
fact that reindeer herders nowadays seldom stay out for long
periods of time. Usually they return to their homes for the
night, even if it requires driving several kilometers. With the
men home every night, there is a net increase in the time spent
in social interaction with people in the household, as well as
with neighbors who may drop in for a visit. All trips to neighbors and to more distant families can be made much more
quickly now than they were formerly, and the Skolts appear
to have used this technological factor to increase wintertime
interpersonal contacts. During the winter of 1966–67, movies
were held biweekly at one of the local homes—an innovation

that would scarcely have been possible in earlier times, since it was not possible to accumulate enough people for such a commercial venture except under fairly unusual circumstances, such as the Easter holidays.

At this time it is difficult to predict what the further effects of the increased intensity of social interaction will be, but the entire economic system now appears to depend on a much faster flow of information than was formerly the case. The speed-up of social contacts (as well as the rapid spread of telephone service to all the neighborhoods) is therefore a necessary concomitant of the new technology. Secondary effects of increases in social interaction are sometimes quite subtle and diffuse. Therefore, specialized research, perhaps over a long period of time, may be essential in order to trace these further ramifications of the snowmobile.

CHAPTER TEN

Technology and Social Change: Summary and Conclusions

In all parts of the world the processes of modernization generally involve complex interactions of technology, commerical systems, governmental policies, population changes, and other factors. It is therefore practically impossible to assign unique "causal efficacy" to any *one* element such as a technological device. Nevertheless, it is possible to study in detail the circumstances of first adoption, early use, and later developments of a new technological item, in order to put together a complex of circumstantial evidence about its effects on peoples' lifeways. That is what I have tried to do in this study. The information in this book is intended, therefore, to provide a credible argument concerning the impact of the snowmobile in one particular ecological context. My suggestions about possible effects in other kinds of ecological contexts are also based on concrete data, but on data which are to a considerable degree less complete.

The main effects of the snowmobile that emerge from my research can be summarized under two general descriptive concepts which I have labeled "de-localization" and "techno-economic differentiation."

De-localization

"De-localization" summarizes in a single term a large number of interrelated processes that make up the main elements of "modernization" all over the world—particularly in previously nonindustrialized (and "non-Westernized") societies. That is to say, the various social and economic aspects of "modernization" are best understood in terms of a very generalized loss of local autonomy through the growth of dependence on a worldwide system of resource allocation and political power. A central feature of the process of delocalization is the growth of *dependence on commercially distributed sources of energy.* It cannot be too strongly emphasized that the sources of energy for maintaining a particular socioeconomic system may provide the best indication of its degree of dependence on the world outside the local area.

In the case of the Skolt Lapps, the socioeconomic system had already been dependent for centuries on *some* material goods from the outside world; and contacts with governmental officials, clergymen, and other outsiders played a significant role in their adaptations to the Suenjel environment. Nonetheless, the energy sources on which they depended most heavily and directly were concentrated in the local environment. Most of their caloric intake came from the reindeer, fish, other game, and vegetation available within their own territories. Flour, sugar, and other foods, as well as various metal goods, were obtained from the Russian trading posts; but the contacts and interdependences with the cash-using outside world constituted only nominal dependence on outside energy sources. The *production equipment* (particularly transportation equipment) that was essential for their subsistence was *powered wholly from local sources of energy.* Thus, if contact with the outside world were cut off at any time, their economic system could have continued to operate fully and effectively (although people would have had to tighten their belts quite a bit).

Throughout the twentieth century the dominant society (first Russian and then Finnish) has impinged more and more directly on Skolt Lapp lifeways. Their dependence on goods and services from afar has increased enormously. However, until the 1960s their principal economic pursuits were still fishing and herding, and the crucial energy sources for operating the system were available mainly within the local environment. Then came the snowmobile and, for the first time, the most critical link in the techno-economic system—the means of transportation—became dependent on outside sources of fossil-fuel energy.

The machines themselves represent very heavy involvement in the outside world and reflect the effects of energy expended at manufacturing plants, but the additional dependence on the outside world that requires our special attention is the fact that the local economic system cannot operate unless it is regularly supplied with gasoline. It is no longer possible to return to a reindeer sled transportation system in the event that gasoline supplies are cut off. The draught reindeer have, for the most part, been sold or killed; and apparently the herding conditions that were integrated with the draught reindeer power system are not likely to be re-instituted. The men still have their skis and use them in some sectors of herding, but it is difficult to imagine that the Lapps could manage all their transportation needs (including freight and wood hauling) with an energy system based on human muscle alone.

For the Skolt Lapp economy, the cost of converting to a fossil fuel energy system has been very high. This cost cannot be paid from local resources but must be subsidized from the outside, in part in the form of transfer payments of pensions, welfare, family bonuses, veterans benefits, and the like. The structuring of the new interdependence with outside energy sources involves the Skolt Lapps and their neighbors in a "whole new ball game" of resource management and manipulation of the socioeconomic network. Effective resource management under these new conditions requires a great many skills and activities, including reading and writing, which are unequally distributed among the families of the region. More important, the skills and activities depend for their exercise on a greatly enlarged technological inventory, of which snowmobiles are only the most conspicuous and perhaps most costly feature. Those families that do not have a full technological inventory, plus a sufficiently high level of knowledge, skills, and information inflow, are very seriously handicapped in all aspects of economic and social adaptation. They are reduced to a passive dependency on the relatively generous Finnish system of social welfare, including the quite effective unemployment programs (temporary work, training programs, and per diem compensation).

I am not suggesting that it is necessarily "a bad thing" for the peoples of the world to be dependent on nonlocal sources of energy and on all the commercial, political, and other systems that follow along the pathways of energy distribution. Life would be hard indeed for the Lapps if they had to return to a state of semi-autonomy of energy sources. The main point to be made is that, with the snowmobile revolution, the Lapps have joined the growing numbers of people for whom a return to energy autonomy is nearly impossible.

Techno-Economic Differentiation

Everyone is familiar with the idea of socioeconomic differentiation, so the concept of "techno-economic" differentiation can be easily understood by analogy. What I want to focus on in using this slightly awkward but expressive terminology is that, for any socio-physical environment, adaptation is effected by means of material things—technological inventories—which are the items of equipment that each individual or household must own or have access to in order to accomplish their food-getting and other subsistence activities. The ownership and utilization of these technological items is closely intertwined with the less material aspects of economic systems—the occupations, the cash reserves, the distributive connections—in terms of which some families and individuals (and other units) are relatively successful in fulfilling their material needs while others experience varying degrees of deprivation.

In the case of the Skolt Lapps the general outlines of the techno-economic requirements should be clear from the descriptions of reindeer herding and other activities in the preceding chapters. The material inventories plus economic and social connections necessary for effectiveness in the environment of northeastern Lapland have changed radically as a result of the new de-localization of energy and related factors brought on by the snowmobile.

The "Material Style of Life" index, presented as Appendix C, inventories a series of items that represent the increasing "technification" of household management in the Sevettijärvi region. It is important to note that the households which do not have the major items (particularly motor saws and snowmobiles) do not usually persist in the utilization of an earlier, pre-snowmobile technology. The people without snowmobiles do not use reindeer sled transportation, and few of the people who lack chain saws persist in cutting firewood by hand. Rather, they are dependent on the people with equipment from whom they hire or borrow the necessary services. Thus, the people who cannot afford full technological inventories constitute a collection of "have nots" who must pay cash to meet their transportation needs and who must adjust their highly dependent household economies to the needs and time schedules of those to whom they turn for these services. This dependence is part of what is meant by the expression, "loss in adaptive flexibility." The reader who scans the list of households with snowmobiles will be somewhat misled by the fact that nowadays very few families lack these machines. The more important facts to note are: a) some families were able to acquire the equipment only very recently (and may lose it if they cannot make the payments); and b) these economically marginal families may often lack both the experience and the finances for keeping the machines operating.

Individuals who do not have readily available transportation (and information inputs) operate at a serious disadvantage, given the present state of the economic situation in northeastern Lapland. It is for this reason that we find some families now maintaining two snowmobiles, so that they will nearly always be able to travel even if one machine breaks down.

Material Possessions and Social Distinctions

The items in the Material Style of Life index are not all equally important for success in the new conditions. Oil heaters and gas fixtures are not really significant technical aids to effective adaptation. On the other hand, those possessions that seem to be simply frosting on the cake, such as telephones and automobiles, confer adaptive advantages on the individuals who can afford to acquire and maintain them. These material possessions have several effects. Beyond the matter of simple technical efficiency, the functions of the items certainly carry over into two related realms that are very difficult to assess— personal esteem and general social prestige.

Techno-economic sufficiency and personal self-esteem appear to have some rather close and interesting interrelationships, for which we unfortunately do not have sufficient data from the Skolt Lapp community. My feeling is that the men and women who have been, in effect, forced out of reindeer-herding activities, which formerly were a chief source of pride and identity, now exhibit some subtle signs of self-loss. Obvious marks of deterioration, such as serious alcoholism, family disorganization, and violent crimes, have not appeared, however. The signs that do appear are mainly in the form of withdrawal—a pulling back from involvement in the action.

One of the clearest expressions of the relationships between technology and prestige is in the pervasive denigration of the ski-men's herding activities. Even the staunchest anti-snowmobile herdsmen admit to a feeling of inferiority in dealing with the machine men. The general mobility and speed that the snowmobile confers is so overwhelming that the costs and possible side effects are easy to ignore. The powerful emotional appeal of the machine is vividly expressed in this essay titled "The Snowmobile in Lapland," by a twelve-year-old boy:

> Reindeer men often use snowmobiles. Here in Lapland it is the favorite means of transportation. The snowmobile is fast. It catches up with a reindeer very quickly. In buying a snowmobile one considers its usefulness in the backwoods. Here the reindeer are certainly gathered when the reindeer men have snowmo-

biles. We also have snowmobile races here. These are for recreation. The snowmobile is also a work vehicle. With it one hauls wood and other materials. Most people drive to roundups by snowmobile, since it would be very far on foot. Here there are snowmobiles in nearly every home. It seems as though it is the best means of transportation.

Seppo Sverloff, Grade IV

The schoolchildren's unqualified admiration for the new machines is a fairly accurate reflection of the predominant opinion in the region, and both schoolchildren and grownups are well aware of who the leading snowmobile owners are.

Social differentiation among the Skolt Lapps has not proceeded very far as yet, but the trends are quite clear. Some families have recently built substantial additions to the two-room cabins that were once so nearly identical in structure. Household furnishings and equipment are being "modernized" quite rapidly in some of the households, while the poorer families make do with what are now somewhat deteriorated reminders of the earlier period of nonmodernized simplicity.

Patterns of social interaction, visiting, and some other aspects of behavior do not reflect any sharp distinctions or growth of "class consciousness," however. Visiting and other social interactions among the Lapps have always been rather informal and flexible, and remain basically egalitarian in tone. The more affluent Finnish families in the area are a little more exclusive in their social behavior, but this is not a recent development. In fact, the social separation between Lapps and Finns has broken down somewhat because of the fact that four of the families in the school complex are composed of "mixed marriages" between Finns and Lapps. Examination of the data in Appendix C shows that at least in material style of life there are no large differences between Finns and Lapps in the Sevettijärvi area, although the two Finnish storekeepers have maintained a position of affluence that is beyond the reach of most other families of the region.

If the people themselves do not make invidious distinctions in terms of the economic, material, and occupational differentiations I have outlined, then what social reality can we

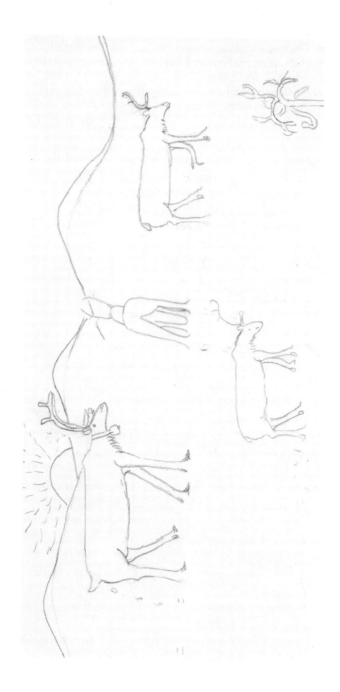

Drawn by Reijo Semenoff, age 9.

Drawn by Rauno Semenoff, age 12.

Drawn by Liisa Marja Ala-Kahrakuusi, age 7.

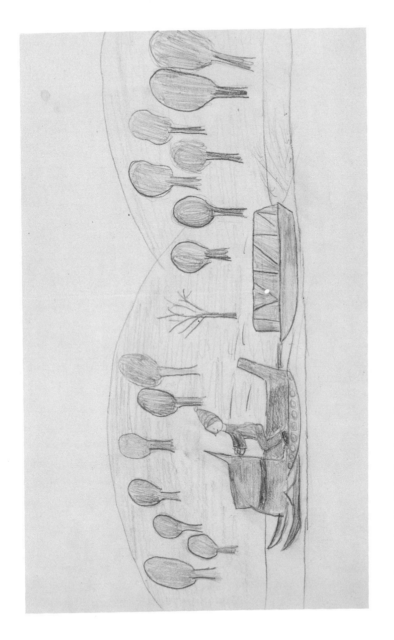

Drawn by Tuula Ala-Kahrakuusi, age 9.

Drawn by Taisto Porsanger, age 9.

claim for these apparently growing distinctions? The practical significance of these facts, as I have already suggested, is that some families and individuals in the Sevetijärvi region are now in a position to take advantage of new resources, new occupational and entrepreneurial niches in the developing techno-economic and social system. Other people have been pushed into a position in which they have very little prospect of gaining economic flexibility, since the adaptive alternatives in Lapland now require financial means, a costly technological inventory, *and* the social connections that come with these resources.

I must repeat again that the social differentiation has not progressed very far as yet, compared to situations in other parts of the world. And there is very little in the way of speech style, clothing, or other status indicators to emphasize techno-economic differentials.

Recently I spoke with the forest ranger in Sevettijärvi about the need for a full-time, fully equipped repair service for both snowmobiles and automobiles. He agreed that it is high time for such an enterprise and suggested that one of the local men will probably attempt such a business venture rather soon. It is not surprising that the two prospects he suggested for this potentially money-making enterprise are fully employed, economically successful young men from the most affluent of the Skolt Lapp families.

Technological Innovation and Social Differentiation

The data on the snowmobile revolution in Sevettijärvi can be looked at in relation to our general hypothesis about the effects of powerful technological inputs in small, modernizing social systems. As diagrammed in Figure 10, the hypothesis is that important technological innovations lead to de-localization and techno-economic differentiation within the community. In time this differentiation brings about visible socioeconomic stratification, which has far-reaching effects on individuals' adaptive skills and opportunities. This hypothesis needs to be examined with data about effects of the snowmo-

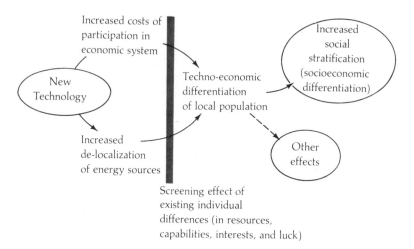

Increased costs of participation in economic system

New Technology

Increased de-localization of energy sources

Techno-economic differentiation of local population

Increased social stratification (socioeconomic differentiation)

Other effects

Screening effect of existing individual differences (in resources, capabilities, interests, and luck)

Figure 10. Hypothesis regarding the effect of new technology upon a small social and economic system.

bile in other arctic areas. (Some data about the introduction of snowmobiles in the North American arctic are presented in Appendix B. However, these materials are very preliminary, and we need a great deal of research before we will have a fuller picture of the transportation revolution in the Alaskan and Canadian arctic.) Of course, the general hypothesis is not limited to the effects of snowmobiles or even of transportational devices, but is proposed as a process that is likely to occur when *any* major contemporary technological innovation transforms a local economic system.

General Conclusions

An ecological study of the snowmobile revolution in northeastern Lapland involves us in a complex interaction of two main lines of theoretical material. On one hand, we have the clear emergence of "techno-environmental causation." The evidence is strong that the introduction of a new technological device in a socioeconomic system has produced very extensive direct and indirect modifications of work patterns, household maintenance systems, and other aspects of adaptive behavior.

At the same time we are confronted with the inescapable importance of *individual differences* (in both physical and psychological characteristics) as factors affecting the adaptive strategies that are played out in the ongoing social action. The growing techno-economic differentiation of Skolt Lappish families and the continuing movement toward a complex stratification, replacing their formerly egalitarian social order comes about through interaction between these two realms of information. If our main interest is in finding out about the kinds of things that produce techno-economic and social stratification, then we need to focus our attention on technological and environmental information to a very considerable extent.

If we direct our theoretical and practical concerns to the prediction and explanation of differential successes and failures in a changing social scene, we should look closely at data about individuals, their information-processing capabilities, and their different decision-making styles. Often, these latter questions are crucially important if one is trying to prevent the development and spread of social pathologies such as crime and psychological disorder.

In the network of information concerning technological and social developments in Lapland, there are no "causal arrows." There are only things and events, with people acting in relation to environmental factors in order to fulfill their psycho-biological needs. The powerful importance of technology and physical environment as factors impinging on human adaptations seems to me beyond dispute, but that does not provide us with sufficient theoretical justification to disregard the ideational and emotional side of the adaptive equation. Neither "techno-economic determinism" nor "cultural causation" provides an adequate model for the complex feedback of effects in the human adaptational system.

To my way of thinking, the juxtaposition of techno-environmental and "mentalistic" causation is precisely where the logic of an ecological approach must lead us. The complex of interactive forces in the behavioral field includes *all* these extra-personal elements—physical and social environment, technolgoical inputs, social organization, idea systems, *and* the bio-psychological characteristics of individuals. Since the ecological frame of reference puts the focus on adaptation—and adaptation finally comes down to the survival and coping effectiveness of *individuals*—then the variations in behavioral characteristics and capabilities of these individuals must be of very great importance for our understanding of outcomes in the study of social change.

The physical fitness of individuals is certainly of concern, and we need much more data on physical functioning in modernizing populations (for example, in relation to diet, disease, etc.); but it has long been claimed that it is man's mental capacities, much more than his physique as such, that has been paramount in the expansion of the species *Homo sapiens* into ever-differentiating ecological niches. The mental characteristics that have been singled out as particularly significant have often focused on sheer "genius" and complexity of technical and symbolic organization, but several other qualities warrant careful attention.

Besides cunning and a very high capacity for storing useful information, successful types of *Homo sapiens* have also exhibited other interesting traits, which apparently vary widely depending on the environmental and technical situations in which they have been put to the test. In some areas of food cultivation brash physical and mental aggressiveness may have shown to advantage, especially in environments where compactness of subsistence resources put considerable numbers of people into close competition. On the other hand, the personal characteristics most favorable to survival in the long grind of persistence hunting (as in the Kalahari Desert and other relatively unfruitful places) would be less likely to include a quickness to combat, and more likely to favor dogged patience accompanied by careful attention to physical detail that alone will lead to ultimate success in bringing down elusive game. Among the Lapps qualities of independent self-reliance, attunement to physical environment, and maintenance of high activity levels have been conducive to adaptive success.

These are much debated points, to be sure; but there seems little dispute that, in general, man's mental characteristics have often been the nexus of his adaptive story, even though we must immediately grant that these psychological attributes, along with their social concomitants, have been operative within the constraints of a techno-environmental framework. Thus I am, after all, granting a kind of materialist primacy to the technical and economic factors—that is what this book is about. But the outcomes, in terms of the individual differences in success stories that are the stuff of adaptation, cannot be understood until we know very much more than is now available about the individual response characteristics of both "winners" and "losers" in man's brisk and self-imposed race to modernization.

CHAPTER ELEVEN

Epilogue

Thus far in this book I have tried as much as possible to present an objective picture of the events and situations that have developed in northeast Finnish Lapland in connection with the spread of the snowmobile. Some parts of the story are quite clear and beyond dispute; others are certainly open to reinterpretation and modification from further information-gathering. We never have enough information to draw final, irrevocable conclusions about things of great technological and social complexity, and there is always more than one way to interpret the information that is available.

Therefore, the statement that I will set forth here must be looked upon as one observer's carefully considered *opinion* with reference to the snowmobile revolution. Others will certainly come to different conclusions, although I hope everyone who expresses himself on these matters does so only after attempts to examine the available facts. The following suggestions are not intended to provide a comprehensive program for change in northeastern Lapland. Rather, I am offering some ideas concerning important points that have come into focus in connection with my research, particularly with reference to the community of Sevettijärvi Skolt Lapps.

It is, of course, impossible to devise programs or suggest policies that would apply homogeneously to the Skolt Lapp people, since they are a differentiated population with a wide variety of different interests, different techno-economic positions, and different modes of adaptation to "modernization." "The average Skolt Lapp" is a fictional abstraction, just as my generalizations about Skolt Lapps as fishermen, parents, and other types of protagonists are all abstractions from the rich variety of human responses. In any case, my main concern in this discussion is with the snowmobile, its impact and relationships to reindeer herding, and the possible future consequences for reindeer husbandry and related activities. Therefore, the suggestions will be of little significance for those many Skolt Lapps and others in the region who nowadays are not interested or concerned with reindeer herding as an economic pursuit.

One of the main assumptions that should be clear at the outset is that I am most concerned about the welfare of the Skolt Lapps as a community of people occupying a particular social and ecological niche. I am less concerned at this point with the economic efficiency *as such* of reindeer herding, and I am not interested in the "preservation of Lappish culture" simply for the sake of preserving "interesting traditions." Skolt Lappish "culture" is worth preserving mainly in terms of its usefulness as an adaptive system for the people who are now identified as Skolt Lapps, and I am not assuming anything about the importance of Skolt Lappish culture in the abstract. Nor am I concerned for the moment with the niceties of Finnish national existence and the betterment of the Finnish people as a citizenry. My statements here thus reflect a concern with bettering the conditions of life in a particular localized area for a particular identifiable group of people. This focus on the welfare of Skolt Lapps does not, however, lead me to suggest policies or programs or solutions that would be clearly detrimental to the interests of other people in that Lappish region. The judgments are intended to strike a fair balance between Skolt Lappish welfare and "fair treatment" for other involved populations.

A second principal assumption I am making is that reindeer herding provides an important, if secondary, source of economic sustenance for a number of people in the Sevettijärvi region, and that this is a useful and dignified occupation which produces food and other materials useful to man not only in the region but in other areas to which reindeer products are exported. Therefore, one basic theme in my discussion is that the reindeer industry should continue to be strong in the Sevettijärvi area.

In the Sevettijärvi school, the boys have from time to time been asked about their role models and occupational aspirations. The overwhelming result is that the boys, with very few exceptions, want to be reindeer herders. When they finish their schooling, not all of them become herders, nor would it be desirable for them to do so, since only a limited number of new participants can be absorbed no matter how the work is organized. Nonetheless, I am assuming that it is psychologically healthy as well as practical that some of the local Lapp boys go into reindeer herding as an adult occupation, since this is an activity that is associated positively with male role models of the area, is a reasonably productive activity, and involves a very considerable amount of personal independence and freedom. The suggestions that follow are intended to fit with some of these value judgments.

1. A viable and productive reindeer-herding industry in the Skolt Lappish area appears to be more likely to continue if the Skolt Lapps have their own reindeer association. In 1969 the separate Näätämö association was formed by dividing the Muddusjärvi association into two equal parts. There are difficulties in this division, particularly for the men at the western end (in the remaining Muddusjärvi district). Nonetheless, aside from some possible redrawing of boundaries in a minor way, I feel that the presence of this separate association is likely to lead to beneficial effects for reindeer herding of the area. Such beneficial consequences are contingent, however, on certain additional factors.

2. Probably the most important prerequisite for the successful maintenance of the separate Näätämö association would be to build a fence separating their reindeer operations from those of the Muddusjärvi people. At the present time there has been some escalation of ill will and herding complications between these two groups, and, unfortunately, there do

not appear to be easy pathways toward more amicable relationships. The conflicts of interest between the "westerners"
and the "easterners" are real, based on some of the ecological
and geographical factors that I have pointed to earlier in this
work. The best way, I feel, to eliminate some of these inter-
group conflicts is to separate their economic interests—their
reindeer herds—with a fence. "Good fences make good neighbors" according to some people. In this instance I am in agreement with that adage.

I am aware that many people argue that the "natural"
habits of the reindeer herds in the Muddusjärvi-Näätämö area
require migrations back and forth across the two districts. My
view of this is that there are no "natural" migration patterns
of reindeer in Finnish Lapland *today*. Fences have been built;
reindeer have been moved from one habitat to another; construction of dams has flooded some areas; and other human
actions have modified greatly the habitats of the reindeer in all
parts of Lapland. The reindeer have, in truth, grown accustomed to migrating back and forth across the expanse of Muddusjärvi-Näätämö territory, but they will adjust their behavior
to new conditions, including new fences, just as reindeer in
most other areas of Lapland have adjusted in the past.

3. Increasing the effectiveness of reindeer operations in
the Näätämö area will require some further modifications in
addition to the interdistrict fence. Modern conditions of marketing require that the Näätämö district have a roundup enclosure that is accessible by truck. Finnish meat inspection laws
now require this, and the Näätämö association must build for
themselves such an enclosure in the near future. Furthermore,
the enclosure must be located to provide the possibility of
driving of herds into the corral during the autumn before
snowfall. Effective reindeer husbandry now requires the sale of
slaughter reindeer early in the fall, and the Näätämö reindeer
herders will need to develop techniques whereby they can get
reindeer to the corral in time to take advantage of premium
meat prices and premium condition of their livestock.

Late summer-fall roundups for commercial purposes
could be of great importance in reducing what appears to be
the detrimental effects of snowmobile herding. Effective gath-

ering of herds in the fall could eliminate the necessity for most of the winter roundups, which seem to be responsible for some physical damage to the reindeer, including reductions in calf production.

4. Some of the Skolt Lapp reindeer herders will strongly disagree with me, but I think that it would be advisable to attempt a return to nonmechanized reindeer herding. If the Skolt Lapps could regain control over their herds, partly through the construction of a fence separating them from their neighbors, it seems possible that they could reinstitute at least partial family control of reindeer herding. A full return to the old winter herding groups and spring calving is no doubt impossible. But the Skolt herds have dwindled to such an extent that they may now be able to maintain a small number of separate herds in selected locations within the district, which could in time be "tamed" to such an extent that cows could again be tied during the spring calving season. Even if this degree of domestication and control cannot be achieved, it seems to me likely that a return to nonmechanized herding methods could result in an improvement in the health of the herds, especially in terms of the weight of the animals and the annual percentages of viable calves.

A strategy of "de-mechanization" of herding would need to include at least a partial restoration of intensive interactions between men and animals—in the form of long-term tending of winter herds. A progressive "gentling" of the animals would require great patience and skill, with an interim period of unproductive trial-and-error "negotiations" between the ski-men and their reindeer. The process by which the Skolts controlled and habituated their newly acquired reindeer herds after the war provides a partial model for this reestablishment of organization.

It should be remembered that a contributing factor of great importance in the worsening reindeer situation of the 1960s has been the deterioration of lichen grounds. Finnish agricultural agents and others have been experimenting with supplemental feeding for reindeer in order to lessen the threat of overgrazing; and the rising price of reindeer meat makes extensive feeding more economically feasible than it has been

Photo 7.   The re-taming of reindeer would require a return to the close interaction between the Lapps and their animals.   *(author)*

in the past. These developments could be of great significance to the future of herding in the Sevettijärvi area. Hand-feeding animals (with bread and other delicacies) has been one of the Skolt Lapps' favorite methods of taming reindeer and could assume importance on a larger scale with new kinds of fodder.

Large-scale supplemental feeding was not logistically feasible in pre-snowmobile days because the modest carrying capacity of the reindeer sled transportation system could not be stretched to carry large amounts of fodder into the backland herding areas. Now, however, there is a large surplus carrying capacity (underutilized snowmobiles) available for such a program. Thus, the snowmobile will certainly be an integral part of any reindeer husbandry system that is developed in the Sevettijärvi area. My suggestions concerning a return to non-mechanized herding apply only to the direct use of machines in driving and rounding up animals.

These proposals concerning "re-taming" the reindeer and establishing more intensive man-animal contacts are not completely strange to contemporary thinking among the Skolt Lapps. In fact, two of them are at present attempting on a small scale to establish control over a few animals through feeding and surveillance. Their efforts seem likely to end in frustration, however, given the fact that they are just two individuals with a few animals trying to maintain islands of control in the midst of the larger mass of uncontrolled reindeer.

It may be quite difficult to begin again to gather animals without vehicles. The reindeer certainly appear to be wild and uncontrollable. However, one of the important factors in herding in the Sevettijärvi area which has not been given sufficient attention, either by the herdsmen or in my discussion here, is the use of herd dogs. Some of the herding failures in recent times—for example, the attempts to gather reindeer in the more rugged sections of the territory—appear to suffer from lack of effective canine help. Any effort to return the herding situation to nonmechanized conditions should be accompanied by a serious attempt to develop a new generation of reindeer dogs. This would require procuring expensive dogs from more southerly reindeer districts and would need financial support from the reindeer association or from some other source. Purchasing and training individual reindeer dogs is a risky and expensive business for individuals to undertake, and it should be underwritten by some kind of organization that is able to spread the investment risks and costs.

5. It is important to consider what kind of a role is possible for reindeer husbandry within the general Sevettijärvi region. Even with rises in the price of reindeer meat (reindeer meat prices have risen by 100 to 150 percent in recent years) and improved efficiencies of herding activity, we cannot expect that herding could ever again become a mainstay of the Skolt Lapp economy. However, the reindeer-herding system in the past had the notable feature of providing a partial economic base for practically every household and, at the same time, insuring a relatively high protein intake into diets—a protein intake that is not easily replaced except at rather great expense, given local conditions. Although only a minority of families in the Sevettijärvi region can ever again expect to support themselves from reindeer herding, it is not beyond the realm of

reason to suggest that reindeer herding should function to provide a substantial portion of the meat protein essential to adequate nutrition in this population. The reindeer meat that is produced through the activities of the minority of reindeer herding families should be available cheaply to the nonherding families of the region, either through their ownership of "shares" in a cooperative enterprise or through association policies of meat sales to residents of the region. Such a policy of low-priced meat sales in the local area could, of course, be supported by governmental funds and policy and would not be contrary to the already widespread effects of the social welfare benefit system of Finland.

For that minority of people of the Sevettijärvi region who will be able to specialize in reindeer-herding activities and ownership, it now appears possible to develop an efficient herding system which would rely on snowmobiles *only for logistic support rather than primary herding,* and which is organized for optimal articulation to the national and international system of meat distribution. Such a herding system will never again require more than a few months of activity at most, leaving the participants free to engage in other kinds of economic pursuits for much of the year—particularly in the summertime. At this time the summer calf-marking system appears to be improving in efficiency, but it remains possible that summer calf-marking could be eliminated in favor of some kind of fall and winter marking or spring calving.

Since I have already put myself quite a way out on a limb with suggestions about reindeer herding and snowmobiles that run counter to much opinion in northeastern Lapland, I venture this further proposition: that in spite of the long and, on the whole, successful history of Skolt Lappish individualism of property ownership and decision making, it is now time for the community, or certain segments of it, to organize—to pool the risks and resources crucially involved in certain aspects of their social and economic system. The Näätämö association, I feel, could begin to play a larger role in the local scene by developing certain essential services, such as a repair service for snowmobiles and possibly a system of cooperative purchasing of snowmobiles and spare parts. As matters now stand in the

Sevettijärvi region, each year a dozen or more new machines are purchased in the local area. These are purchased at full price from the three local dealers. The profits that now accrue to these dealers could as well be transferred in the form of lower costs to the snowmobile operators themselves. Possibly the matter of purchasing new machines is not as important as the provision of spare parts and repair service.

Most of the suggestions that I have outlined here have relatively little chance of adoption. To be sure, the policies of the Finnish government are likely to include the continuance of the separate fledgling Näätämö association. In time, this association will build a roundup enclosure with an access road and other features essential to modern reindeer marketing. The possibilities of getting a fence built between the Näätämö and Muddusjärvi associations seem more remote at the present time, since it is actively opposed by the Muddusjärvi reindeer men. Also the policies of the Union of Reindeer Associations are not particularly favorable to the building of more and more fences restricting the movement of the animals.

It is nonetheless important for me to set out these ideas in this form, because they express some very important aspects of the reindeer-herding system as an intrinsic segment of the Skolt Lapp way of life. It should not be forgotten that the Skolt Lapps have throughout recent generations identified themselves as reindeer men. Their folklore, their songs, their idle-hour entertainments, and many other aspects of culture have been structured around themes of reindeer herding as a central feature. Identification with an economically successful and important occupation that requires great amounts of knowledge, self-reliance, and resourcefulness on the part of its practicioners has been one of the main strengths of Skolt Lapp adaptation during the recent decades of increasingly rapid social and economic change. Even though increasing numbers of Skolt Lapps have dropped out of reindeer herding (both voluntarily and involuntarily), this activity could still provide a focal point for their identification and self-respect as an identifiable "minority ethnic group" within the larger context of the Finnish national social system. No one pretends that Skolt Lapps will continue forever to maintain their own language and carry on a traditional way of life—whatever that might mean. But reindeer herding can be a modern and even lucrative occupation. And it does not appear that the long-range productiveness of the reindeer industry is advanced by snowmobilized herding, at least not in the Sevettijärvi area.

Moving from the specifics of mechanized reindeer herding to a larger perspective, I want to raise one further practical suggestion—or at least a question—which I will present here as a "legal brief":

1. Whereas the rapid spread of snowmobiles in Lapland and in northern North America has brought about widespread changes in economic and social organization and appears to have very important ecological consequences;

2. And whereas the spread of this technological device and many others of like nature have been brought about through the operation of the general "free enterprise" system of commercial distribution;

3. And whereas in the usual case of such commercial products *there is no point in the distributional process* in which the receiving public—the consumers and their neighbors—can study, discuss, and debate the possible future outcomes and "vote on" whether it is wise to allow a particular multi-effect technological event to proceed unchecked;

4. Be it resolved that nations, regions, and perhaps even local communities should have the opportunity to hear expert testimony and all other pertinent information concerning new technological devices, including the presentation of arguments by the potential commercial distributors and the opposition; from which information and argument the affected population (of whatever size and region) can decide —through a duly selected commission, legislative body, or direct popular vote—whether the new technological feature should be allowed onto the open market;

5. That in those cases where technological innovations are seen to provide many positive features, supposedly justifying their acceptance by the affected population, the product be taxed and regulated to the extent necessary to provide safeguards against negative side effects and to defray costs of adjustments to those portions of the population and natural environments that are negatively affected—through technological unemployment, localized ecological damage, and other kinds of losses.

6. *Discussion.* This type of procedure (of debate and study) *is* carried out in the case of most large-scale, publicly financed technological developments—dams, roads, sewer systems, public buildings. In addition zoning laws, the increasing numbers of pollution control regulations, and other public legislation give recognition to the *need for choice and decision* in connection with big technology. Food and drug laws and related health legislation do, of course, provide for some consideration of the direct health-related effects of commercial products; but these controls do not reach out to consider the possible social and ecological ramifications of new devices and products.

Consider for a moment what some of the world's environments and social systems *might* be like if the affected people had had a well-informed chance to "vote on" the introduction of rifles into plains buffalo hunting, or on the uncontrolled use of various powerful and dangerous pesticides, or the spread of high-speed motorboats on the recreational lakes of North America, and so on. Of course, in most cases the people could not possibly have had enough information about all of the secondary effects of the technological innovations; and they would, no doubt, have voted to accept what seemed at the time to be reasonably "useful" and productive "technical advances." At the same time, careful consideration of these kinds of items *before* they become widespread could bring about some earlier recognition of the need for caution and countermeasures to diminish their apparently negative side effects.

I realize that setting up the machinery and working principles for this "ecological review" procedure would be an extremely difficult task. How would the "ecological review" procedure be initiated? How would various segments of the public and government be represented? How would they generate the necessary information to make decisions? Etc. Etc. . . .

In principle, however, my suggestion is not so different from those other kinds of review situations mentioned above—for example the hearings concerned with large-scale modifications of the environment. We need to develop new procedures and new decision-making in *all* areas of technological development if human populations, large and small, are to maintain some control over their local physical and economic environments.

APPENDIX A

Notes on
Research Methods

The credibility of the information and argument that I have presented in this book rests principally on my personal observations of events and people in northeastern Finnish Lapland during several periods of fieldwork beginning in 1958 and including my most recent trip in the summer of 1971. My earliest fieldwork (resulting in my Ph.D. dissertation, University of California, Berkeley; 1960) involved very considerable participation in reindeer-herding activities over a period of fifteen months. During that time I attended nearly a dozen reindeer roundups, assisted herdsmen in spring calving operations, traveled with reindeer men in the fall roundup of geldings, spent time with the association winter herd, and talked with Skolt Lapps and other herdsmen on innumerable occasions about details of reindeer activities. I have well over a thousand photographs from those early periods of fieldwork, and scanning them helps me to recall some important details of those earlier events.

My later periods of fieldwork in Lapland have involved less direct participation in activities, and rather more time in interviewing as well as collecting quantified data. In the summer of 1962, I collected about fifty responses to a projective test (a set of pictures) that I had devised with the artistic and technical help of Robert J. Maxwell. Five years later (1967) I again had the opportunity to visit the Sevettijärvi region for a

brief period, this time concentrating my interviewing and observations on the snowmobiles. In a few weeks I interviewed
almost all the snowmobile owners in the local area, as well as
many of the nonowners. The late Pekka Moshnikoff took me
to two roundups, in which I had the opportunity to participate
directly in "snowmobilized" reindeer drives.

I had hired an able Finnish linquist-enthnographer, Pekka
Sammallahti, to assist me in data gathering during this early
work on the snowmobile, and Martti Linkola of the University
of Jyväskylä helped in drafting and circulating questionnaires
to all the reindeer associations in Finland. (He got a remarkable
100 percent return on these question schedules!) Our continued work on the snowmobile problem has involved a continuing correspondence across the Atlantic, as new information
appeared and as we prepared our first report on these studies
(Pelto, Linkola, Sammallahti, 1968).

Arto Sverloff agreed to work for me as research assistant
in 1962 and again in the summer of 1971. Together we visited
most of the Skolt Lapp households, gathering data through
both structured instruments and informal interviewing. Arto
also spent many hours in answering my questions, studying
maps and diagrams, and reflecting on some of the preliminary
generalizations that I wrote up. This last procedure I feel is
highly productive—the anthropologist generates preliminary
hypotheses and statements; the informant-assistant comments
and corrects; then both go out to gather more data in the
community.

Some people who know my prejudices and concerns about
ethnographic methodology will be surprised to learn that I
relied to a considerable extent on a rather small number of key
informants for significant portions of my interviewing data.
For some areas of information about reindeer matters, a key
informant was the only practical way to get extensive, descriptive data. In these cases I relied heavily on persons who were
the most active protagonists in the reindeer-herding events
about which I sought information. This informal interviewing
about past events was often most fruitful when we were actually in some reindeer-herding setting, at a roundup site, sitting
in a backlands reindeer cabin, or traveling in the tundra in

search of geldings. Also, informal interviewing was often directly connected with visits to a series of households—providing for quick feedback of "data quality control."

In general I have tried, wherever possible, to gather quantified data (for example, household inventories, numbers of reindeer, etc.) *and* qualitative data (personal narratives, descriptions of events, statements of opinions) together, so the different types of data make up a system of interrelated parts. I feel that neither the descriptive, "personalized" material nor the numerical information would alone provide a sufficiently credible argument.

Comparisons and Contrasts
in the Snowmobile Revolution:
Some Regional and
Cross-Continental Variations

The purpose of this book has been to present a detailed examination of the effects of the snowmobile on a particular community. Some of the developments among the Skolt Lapps are perhaps unique to their specific environmental situation. On the other hand, I suggest that certain of the effects of mechanization will be broadly similar in a variety of different environments. To test these generalizations (and to study the significance of local variations) we will, of course, need a great deal of detailed information from a number of arctic communities and regions. Some preliminary data are available from several parts of the arctic, and it is worthwhile to briefly examine them here. (These data are included here mainly as brief guidelines for persons interested in further study of the snowmobile revolution.)

The Snowmobile in Utsjoki

The Lapps of Utsjoki, just north of Sevettijärvi, were the first reindeer herders in Finland to experiment with snowmobiles in herding. Their herding area is immediately adjacent to Muddusjärvi and Näätämö, and like their neighbors, they are under the aegis of the Finnish reindeer association system. Utsjoki is the only Finnish commune that has continued to be predominantly Lappish down to modern times. In 1962 the population of Utsjoki was 1233, of which 885 were Lappish; reindeer herding has been almost completely in the hands of the Lapps (Nickul, E. 1968; Müller-Wille and Aikio 1971).

The snowmobile revolution in Utsjoki took a shape quite different in some respects from the processes I have described for Sevettijärvi. The striking contrasts in the impact of mechanization in the two districts serve to underscore some of the ways in which differences in physical and social environment, as well as past cultural history, have powerful effects on the paths of social change.

A major factor in the apparent instant success of snowmobiles in the Kaldoaivi district is the treeless tundra terrain. The open landscape is so favorable to vehicular travel that the herders are now using motorcycles for summer and fall herding! (Müller-Wille and Aikio 1972) The use of the sturdy cross-country Yamaha machines would be unthinkable in most of the forested and rocky Muddusjärvi and Näätämö region. From the very first attempts to herd reindeer by snowmobile (beginning in the winter of 1962–63) the Kaldoaivi Lapps were able to bring their herds to the corrals without serious losses. The effectiveness of their operations is visible in the sizeable herds processed in the roundups that took place in 1968–69. During fieldwork that winter Müller-Wille observed drives in which 2000–3000 animals were successfully brought to the roundup corral without the scattering and disorganization that characterized snowmobile operations in the Muddusjärvi district.

Thus the Kaldoaivi reindeer herds have not become "dedomesticated" to a harmful degree, and the disastrous loss of herds by small owners has not taken place, at least not to the extent that it has among the Sevettijärvi people. Compared to the patterns of mechanized herding in the Muddusjärvi-Näätämö area, the Kaldoaivi herdsmen are able to sweep their district relatively cleanly, so that few reindeer remain unprocessed; they have few unsuccessful roundups; and most of their animals are processed only once in the course of a herding season. As a result their mechanized herding activities do not appear to entail as much harassment of the reindeer as is found in the Näätämö-Muddusjärvi region.

One important difference between the Kaldoaivi and Näätämö herding situations is the fact that the Utsjoki men have been relatively large-scale herders for centuries and have never had the kind of individualized, close interaction with their reindeer that the Skolt Lapps have tried to maintain. For example, calf-marking has been carried out at summer corrals in Utsjoki region for a long time, rather than in the context of spring calving. Thus effective herd maintenance has not been seriously hampered by the fact that the reindeer have become, even in Utsjoki, more estranged from human contact.

The adoption of mechanized herding in Utsjoki has required much less modification of the overall herding structure. On the other hand, it is clear that these are rather extensive economic consequences nonetheless.

It is noteworthy that the wealthier reindeer men of Utsjoki appear to have "overspent" by slaughtering and selling off too many reindeer during the recent period of mechanization. Table 13 shows this pattern, which in the short run would appear to have a "leveling effect" on economic inequalities.

It is probable that the wealthier men of Utsjoki "overspent" in part for purposes other than snowmobile acquisition and maintenance. They have also acquired automobiles, outboard motors, and other kinds of equipment. Since 1968 they have spent extra money to acquire motorcycles for use in summer calving operations and fall (pre-snow) roundups. The prediction for the 1970s is that the men with full equipment—snowmobiles and motorcycles—will control and monopolize herding operations to an increasing degree, gradually freezing out the smaller owners (L. Müller-Wille, personal communication).

The high costs of mechanized operations are reflected (in part) in increases of slaughtering and sales in Kaldoaivi association; and they are very likely to lead to increased consolidation of herding operations in the hands of a small number of wealthy operators, just as in Sevettijärvi.

The matter of physical damage to the reindeer from the

Table 13. Patterns of Reindeer Sales and "Net Growth" in Kaldoaivi Association before and after the "Snowmobile Revolution"

Period	Reindeer slaughtered and sold	Net increase in herds
1956–61		
Owner A[a]	25.5%	1.7%
Owner B	15.5	34.3
Owner C	22.7	13.5
Total association (104 members)	23.7%	7.8%
1963–69		
Owner A	43.7%	−16.8%
Owner B	32.6	−17.4
Owner C	42.0	−20.2
Total association (111 members)	32.7%	−10.0%

Source: Muller-Wille and Aiko, 1971.

[a] A, B, and C are the three wealthiest reindeer herders in the association.

quickened tempo of roundups and other actions is difficult to assess, but the statistics on calf production suggest that even in Kaldoaivi there has been some damage to the animals. During the latter part of the 1960s there was a significant decrease in calf percentages (see Figure 7). However, their calves made a sharp comeback in 1969–70. One swallow does not make a summer, and a single excellent year does not prove that the mechanized herders have solved all the problems of strains on the animals. However, it is quite possible that the Kaldoaivi herdsmen's general success in processing their reindeer without having to subject them to repetitious roundups augurs for a pattern of successful husbandry.

Given the advantages for motor vehicles inherent in the Utsjoki landscape, it seems likely that in the long run the mechanization of herding will be economically more profitable than it is in the more difficult terrain immediately to the south. It is certainly instructive that in some of the heavily forested reindeer districts in southern Lapland there is still very little use of snowmobiles in herding operations.

The differences between the Utsjoki and Sevettijärvi adjustments to mechanized herding should not lead us to ignore significant similarities. Consolidation of power and control in the hands of the techno-economic leaders is apparent in both cases, and the out-migration of persons who are now "technologically unemployed" began in Utsjoki before it was noticeable among the Skolt Lapps. In both communities the picture is complicated by the fact that many other factors, such as new roads and the development of tourism, influence the structure of social interactions and distribution of economic possibilities.

The Snowmobile in Arctic North America

In the far north of Canada and Alaska the coming of "the iron dogsled" has been as swift, far-ranging, and varied in its impact as it was in Lapland. In some Eskimo communities the transition from dogsled to snowmobile (or "Ski-Doo") took place in a single year. In the Broughton Island community, for example, a serious epidemic among the sled-dogs (1963) brought about a transportation crisis, for which the advent of the snowmobile was a totally unexpected but successful solution. In 1965, when David Stevenson of Dalhousie University was carrying out research among the Broughton Islanders, only one of the twenty able-bodied hunters still used dogs regularly.

Among the Belcher Island Eskimos, on the other hand, the snowmobile appears to be much more marginal in its economic advantages, particularly because of the rugged sea-ice over which these people must travel in search of game. Also, supplies of gasoline are quite irregular at the trading post, so the hunters who rely on machines may find themselves without means of transportation at crucial times. Lee Guemple, who studied the Belcher Islanders in the late sixties, estimated that the costs of operation of snowmobiles and of sled-dogs were approximately equal—about $3.00 per day. The number of snow vehicles in the community has increased slowly during recent years, but they do not appear to convey clear economic advantages to the hunters, and the number of breakdowns with the machines has also been a deterrent to widespread adoptions.

At Banks Island, in the western Canadian far north, 1966–67 was a significant turning point in snowmobile use, for most of the trappers in that community had an exceptionally profitable season. In ordering supplies for the following year nearly every man in the community ordered a machine. In spite of the ready adoption of mechanized travel equipment, the Banks Islanders did not give up their dogs, and they frequently bring their animals with them on the traplines as insurance against breakdowns. Geographer Peter Usher, who spent many months among the Banks Island trappers, finds little evidence of any growth of socio-economic differentiation as a result of the machines, and notes that whatever transportation advantages the snowmobiles have brought are generally invested in leisure time rather than in increased economic activity.

Growth of differences between the "haves" and "have nots" seems fairly clear among some Eskimo groups in which there were already clear differentiations between wage earners and full-time hunter-trappers. Lorne Smith carried out a survey of snowmobile costs and utilization among the people of Pond Inlet (Baffin Island) and found that most of the owners of vehicles are wage earners. "For an employed Eskimo, ski-doo ownership makes good sense, because he is able to enjoy the best of two worlds. He is assured of a steady wage from his employment, and at the same time because of the mobility afforded by the ski-doo he does not have to depend on expensive store bought food; he can still obtain a major portion of his food through traditional methods" (Smith, L. 1970b:7). The economic advantages as well as other attractions of snowmobile ownership appear to bestow high prestige on one portion of the population, increasing the differentiation separating the employed people from the non-wage earning, nonmechanized part of the population.

In the community of Aklavik in western Canada, Derek Smith has noted tendencies to increased social separation between the Eskimo elite (wage workers with snowmobiles) and the "bush people." Smith reported that "The snowmobile has introduced a polarization, a differentiation within the community ... which (worsens) ... by relative deprivation, the position of bush-oriented, relatively traditional Eskimo families" (Smith, D. 1970).

On the Alaskan side of the North American arctic the explosive adoption of the snowmobile has similarly led to somewhat differing patterns of economic and social change, depending on local circumstances of physical and social environment. Edwin Hall has described important changes in hunting patterns brought about by conversion to snowmobiles in Noatak, a village of about 250 people. It is interesting to note that extensive adoption of the machines did not occur until the winter of 1966–67, at least six years after snowmobiles first appeared in Kotzebue, the market center about fifty miles from Noatak. In spite of this apparent slowness in acceptance of the new transportation system, "Only one Noatak man used dogs for hunting during the winter of 1969–70 and he purchased a snowmobile in the spring of 1970" (Hall 1971:254).

Karl Francis surveyed the spread of snowmobiles in twenty-seven villages in northern Alaska and found that there was a fivefold increase in machines during the period from 1963 to 1968. In that latter year there were already a total of 974 "mechanical toboggans" in the reporting communities.

Both Francis and Hall predict that the effects of the "iron dog" in northern Alaska will produce very wide-ranging changes beyond the already substantial social transformation they were able to observe in the last years of the sixties. They report general increases in social interaction, greatly heightened dependency on cash incomes, and marked changes in hunting patterns. One of the major changes that has developed as dog teams are replaced is the diminution of hunting and fishing to provision the dogs. Hall feels that the fall salmon fishing by people around Noatak will decline considerably, since much of the salmon catch was previously used for dog food.

The tendencies toward increased socioeconomic inequality appear to be quite noticeable in the Alaskan arctic scene. Hall suggests a "widening economic gap between those who continue to use dog teams and those who have turned to snow-mobiles"; and Francis feels that "more and more the villagers of arctic Alaska seem to be breaking into two distinct groups, the people who have the requisite equipment for a productive hunt and the people who have little but devastating poverty, humiliation, the characteristic charity of their successful neighbors, and the government dole" (Francis 1969:78).

Although I have touched on only the barest details of this transportation revolution, it seems beyond doubt that very major changes in life-styles are coming about because of the introduction of snowmobiles. While certain main trends are discernible in spite of regional and cross-national differences, it is important to note that details of local environment have very strong effects on the ways in which the machines are introduced and adapted to existing sociocultural and techno-logical systems.

Differences in the physical and biological environment are, of course, very significant. In many parts of north Alaska the snowmobiles have enabled people to kill much larger num-bers of caribou for local food consumption. In the eastern arctic in areas where there are few caribou, the hunting advantages of the snowmobile are less clear, since it is not feasible to chase seals and other marine animals with the machines. Trapping economies such as Banks Island represent yet a third type of local man-animal-machine ecological system, in which the snowmobiles provide some added convenience to economic pursuits, but may not bring about marked changes in the struc-turing of economic activities. In Lapland where neither hunt-ing nor trapping are of any consequence, the chief impacts of the machines on economic pursuits are strongly patterned by the habits and reactions of the semi-domesticated reindeer.

Local and regional details of *social* environment are also of great importance in the overall ecological picture. The types and amounts of wage-labor opportunities, relationships among ethnic groups, presence of relatively wealthy representatives of the dominant industrial society, and the structuring of com-mercial operations are a few of the features of social organiza-tion that account for variations in the effects of new technological devices on local populations.

The socioeconomic impact of the snowmobile has been so striking in part because of the centrality of transportation as an element in arctic systems of adaptation. The rapidity of its spread across the arctic, together with the extensiveness of secondary effects, makes it an especially important instance of technological influence on social change.

APPENDIX C

A Scale of
"Material Style of Life"
(Techno - Economic Differentiation)
in Sevettijärvi, Finland

Table C-1. Inventory of Sevettijärvi Households

Key to Items:

    A.   Household owns a chain saw.

    B.   Number of snowmobiles owned.

    C.   Household has a telephone.

    D.   Household owns a washing machine.

    E.   Household uses gas (or electricity) for cooking *or* lighting.

    F.   Household has oil heating.

    G.   Household uses gas (or electricity) for *both* cooking *and* lighting.

    H.   Household owns an automobile.

    I.   Household owns a refrigerator.

    J.   Household owns a television.

Household No.[a]	A.	B.	C.	D.	E.	F.	G.	H.	I.	J.
I F1	x	3	x	x	x	x	x	x	x	x
I 34	x	2	x	x	x	x	x	x	x	x
II F2	x	1	x	x	x	x	x	x	x	
II L1	-	1	x	x	x	x	x	x	x	
II 45	x	1	x	x	x	x	o	x	x	
II 52	-	1	x	x	x	x	x	o	x	
III 28	x	2	x	x	x	x	x	x		
III 53	x	1	x	x	x	x	x	x		
III 54	o	1	x	x	x	x	x	x		
IV 44	x	1	x	x	x	x	x			
IV 12	-	1	x[b]	x	x	o	x			
V L2	x	2	x	-	-	x				
V 55	x	1	x	x	-	x				
V 39	-	2	o	o	x	x				
VI 47	x	2	x	x	x					
VI L3	x	2	x	-	x			x		
VI 42	x	1	x	x	x					
VI 30	x	1	-	x	x					
VI 38	-.	1	x	x	x					
VI 37	x	1	o	x	x			x		
VI 32	x	1	o	x	x					
VI 25	x	1	o	x	x					
VI 13	o	1	x[b]	x	x				x	
VI 11	o	1	o	x	x					
VII 21	x	2	x	x						
VII 7	x	1	x	x						
VII 29	x	1	o	x						
27	x	2	x							
56	x	1	x							
8	x	1	x							
Approximate Median of Skolt Lapp Households										
	x	1	x							
VIII 50	x	1	x[b]							
VIII F3	-	1	x							
VIII L4	-	1	x							
VIII 6	o	1	x							
VIII 17	x	o	x							
VIII F4	x	o	x							
VIII 18	x	o	x[b]							

	Household No.	A.	B.	C.	D.	E.	F.	G.	H.	I.	J.
	43	x	2								
	14	x	2								
	33	x	2								
	F5	-	2								
	F6	x	1								
	57	x	1								
	L5	x	1								
	46	x	1								
	5	x	1								
	L6	x	1								
	10	x	1								
IX	4	-	1								
	F7	-	1								
	F8	-	1								x	
	L7	-	1								
	F9	-	1								
	20	-	1								
	23	-	1								
	40	-	1								
	15	o	1								
	51	o	1								
	35	o	1								
	26	o	1								
	16	x									
	2	x									x
X	31	x									
	24	x									
	F10	x									
	L8	-		x							
	19										
XI	9										
	L9										

Note: The symbol "x" denotes the presence of an item in a household.

The symbol "-" denotes the absence of information about an item.

The symbol "o" denotes the absence of an item in a position in which it constitutes an "error," that is, one would predict the presence of the item, given the other items owned or used by the household.

The absence of an item in a "non-error" position is denoted by a blank space.

[a]Household numbers of one or two digits without a letter prefix signify Skolt Lapp households. The prefix "F" signifies a Finnish household, and the prefix "L" signifies a Lappish, but non-Skolt, household.

[b]The telephones in these houses were installed at the expense of the Finnish government and are used on a cost-per-call basis.

One measure of the reliability of the scale is the percent of error[a], technically referred to as the "coefficient of reproducibility." In this scale there are 678 items (excluding the "no information" items) and twenty-eight errors. Using the formula

$$100 - \frac{\text{Errors}}{\text{Total Number of Items}}$$

the coefficient of reproducibility is .96. A coefficient of .90 or greater is considered to be significantly reliable.

Errors occurred with the following frequency for each item tabulated:

A. Chain saw, 8
B. Snowmobile, 3
C. Telephone, 6
D. Washing machine, 2
E. Gas (cooking or light), 0
F. Oil heat, 1
G. Gas (cooking and light), 1
H. Automobile, 4
I. Refrigerator, 1
J. Television, 2

The data tabulated in Table C-1 can be interpreted as a classification of the Sevettijärvi households according to the items owned or used. Table C-2 gives such a classification, from scale type I (household has all the listed items) to scale XI (household has none of the listed items), for Skolt Lapp, Finnish, and other Lapp households in the Sevettijärvi region.

[a]"Error" refers to deviations from a theoretically "perfect" cumulative scale.

Table C-2.   Classification of Sevettijärvi Households According to "Material Style of Life."

Scale type	Total no. of households	Skolt Lapp households	Finnish households	Other Lapp households	Errors
I	2	1	1	0	0
II	4	2	1	1	2
III	3	3	0	0	1
IV	2	2	0	0	1
V	3	2	0	1	2
VI	10	9	0	1	9
VII	3	3	0	0	1
VIII	11	8	2	1	5
IX	23	15	5	3	5
X	6	4	1	1	2
XI	3	2	0	1	0
Totals	70	51	10	9	28

APPENDIX D

Material Style of Life of the Ten "Top" Reindeer - Herding Households in the Näätämö Association

---

Material Style of Life of the Ten "Top" Reindeer Households in the Näätamö Association

Rank order of herd size	*Material Style of Life*
1	VII
2	II
3	III
4	IX
5	V
6	VII
7	IX
8	VII
9	VIII[a]
10	IV

Note: These are the ten Skolt families in the Näätamö association that still have over thirty-five adult reindeer and have some possibility of re-building their herds. All except the fourth and seventh are in the top half of the Material Style of Life scale.

[a] Although household 9 is in scale type VIII (which includes families below the median in this rank order) they have two snowmobiles and an automobile, so they clearly belong with the more affluent households.

These data show that the households with the larger inventories of material items (techno-economic resources) are the ones that have been able to maintain viable reindeer herds. Thus, the families with greater material resources and greater access to local wage-labor jobs are also the most successful in reindeer husbandry (see footnote to Table 13).

Official Reindeer Tallies
in Northeastern Finnish Lapland

Official Reindeer Tallies in Northeastern Finnish Lapland

	Kaldoaivi	Muddusjärvi	Vätsäri	Skolt Lapps (of Muddusjärvi)
1958–59	5714	6993	4417	
1959–60	5794	6762	4773	
1960–61	8128	8147	4361	2678[a]
1961–62	6833	6761	3575	2167
1962–63	5948	5536	2151	
1963–64	6058	6012	2933	
1964–65	6630	6859	3432	1829
1965–66	5817	4093	1893	
1966–67	3761	4567	2267	1338
1967–68	5923	5618	2890	
1968–69	5110	5388	2582	1498
1969–70	4257	3451[a]	2516	1272(1604)[b]
1970–71				1689

Note: The total tallies of reindeer may be looked upon with some skepticism, since these are the taxable figures and reindeer herders, including the heads of the reindeer associations, have some reason to underestimate the figures from time to time. The fact that each district has an officially allowed top limit to the reindeer tally also occasions some underestimating in the reporting. Also, the thoroughness of reindeer roundups varies a good deal from year to year, especially during the transition to snowmobiles in the 1960s.

[a] The Skolt Lapp reindeer are counted in the Muddusjärvi total until 1969–70. In that year the Skolt Lapp district of Näätamö was officially recognized, so the Muddusjärvi total no longer includes Skolt Lapp reindeer.

[b]For 1969 I have two different figures for the Skolt Lapp total reindeer tally. Since the figure of 1604 was obtained from the chairman of the Näätämö association, it is the more trustworthy. The figures of 1272 was obtained from the Central Union of Reindeer Associations.

Bibliography

CHAPTER ONE

Bennett, John
    1969 *Northern Plainsmen: Adaptive Strategy and Agrarian Life.*
    Chicago: Aldine.

Downs, James F.
    1961 "The Origin and Spread of Riding in the Near East and
    Central Asia." *American Anthropologist* 63:1193-1203.

Geertz, Clifford
    1963 *Agricultural Involution.* Berkeley: University of California
    Press.

Harris, Marvin
    1963 *The Rise of Anthropological Theory.* New York: Thomas
    Crowell.

Rappaport, Roy
    1968 *Pigs for the Ancestors: Ritual in the Ecology of a New
    Guinea People.* New Haven: Yale University Press.

Vayda, Andrew P. (ed.)
    1969 *Environment and Cultural Behavior: Ecological Studies in
    Cultural Anthropology.* Garden City: The Natural History
    Press.

CHAPTER TWO

Fried, Morton
  1967 *The Evolution of Political Society: An Essay in Political Anthropology.* New York: Random House.

Lewin, T., K. Nickul, and A. W. Eriksson
  1970 "Stature and Aging of the Skolt Lapps." *Acta Morphol. Neerl.-Scand.* 8:187–193.

Platt, Raye R. (ed.)
  1955 *Finland and Its Geography.* An American Geographical Society Handbook. New York: Duell, Sloan, and Pearce.

Sahlins, Marshall D.
  1958 *Social Stratification in Polynesia.* Seattle: University of Washington Press.

CHAPTER THREE

Huhtanen, Urpo
  1970 *Porovuosi: Reindeer Year.* Helsinki: Werner Söderström.

Nickul, Karl
  1970 *Saamelaiset Kansana ja Kansalaisina.* Helsinki: Suomalaisen Kirjallisuuden Seura.

CHAPTER FOUR

Itkonen, T. I.
  1948 *Suomen Lappalaiset,* 2 Vols. Porvoo/Helsinki: Werner Söderström.

Pelto, Pertti J.
  1964 "Personality in an Individualistic Society." Paper read at the Annual Meeting of the American Anthropological Association, Chicago, Illinois.

CHAPTER FIVE

Alaruikka, Yrjo
  1964 *Suomen Porotalous* [Reindeer Industry of Finland].

Rovaniemi: Lapin maakuntapaino, Lapland Provincial Press.

Müller-Wille, Ludger
1970 *The Impact of the Snowmobile in Utsjoki, a Lappish-Finnish Community in Northern Finland.* University of Münster, Seminar für Völkerkunde.

Pelto, Pertti J., Martti Linkola and Pekka Sammallahti
1968 "The Snowmobile Revolution in Lapland." *Journal of the Finno-Ugric Society* 69:3–42.

Pelto, Pertti J. and Ludger Müller-Wille
1972 "Snowmobiles: Technological Revolution in the Arctic." In *Technology and Social Change,* edited by H. R. Bernard and P. J. Pelto. New York: Macmillan.

CHAPTER EIGHT

Müller-Wille, Ludger and Olavi Aikio
1971 "Die Auswirkungen der Mechanisierung der Rentierwirtschaft in der lappischen Gemeinde Utsjoki (Finnisch-Lappland)." *Terra* 83:179–185.

Poromies [The Reindeer Man]
Monthly publication of the Union of Reindeer Associations (Paliskuntain Yhdistys), Rovaniemi. [Official reindeer tallies appear annually in the May issue.]

CHAPTER NINE

McClelland, David C.
1961 *The Achieving Society.* (Princeton: Van Nostrand and Co.).

Paine, Robert
1965 *Coast Lapp Society II.* Tromsö: Museums Skrifter IV, 2.

Pelto, Pertti J.
1962 *Individualism in Skolt Lapp Society.* Helsinki: [Finnish Antiquities Society] Kansatieteellinen Arkisto 16.

————, Martti Linkola and Pekka Sammallahti
1968 "The Snowmobile Revolution in Lapland," *Journal of the Finno-Ugric Society* 69:3–42.

————
1971 "Social Uninvolvement and Psychological Adaptation in the Arctic." Paper presented at the Second International Symposium on Circumpolar Health, Oulu, Finland.

APPENDIX B

Francis, Karl E.
1969 "Decline of the Dogsled in Villages of Arctic Alaska: a Preliminary Discussion." In *Yearbook of the Association of Pacific Coast Geographers* 31 (edited by John F. Gaines):69–78.

Hall, Edwin S., Jr.
1971 "The 'Iron Dog' in Northern Alaska." *Anthropologica* XIII (1–2):237–254.

Müller-Wille, Ludger and Pertti J. Pelto
1971 "Technological Change and Its Impact in Arctic Regions: Lapps Introduce Snowmobiles into Reindeer Herding." *Polarforschung* (W. Germany).

Müller-Wille, Ludger and Olavi Aikio
1971 "Die Auswirkungen der Mechanisierung der Rentierwirtschaft in der lappischen Gemeinde Utsjoki (Finnisch-Lappland)." *Terra* 83:179–185.

Nickul, Erkki
1968 "Suomen saamelaiset vuonna 1962" [The Finnish Lapps in 1962]. *Tilastokatsauksia* (Helsinki) 7:59–63.

Smith, Derek
1970 Tape-recorded interview.

Smith, Lorne
1970a Tape-recorded interview.
1970b "The Mechanical Dog Team: The Ski-Doo in the Canadian Arctic." Paper presented at the Tenth Annual

Meeting of the Northeastern Anthropological
Association, Ottawa.

Stevenson, David
1967 Tape-recorded interview.

Usher, Peter
1966 *Banks Island: An Area Economic Survey, 1965.* Report of
the Department of Indian Affairs and Northern
Development. Reprinted 1968.
1968 Tape-recorded interview.
1970a Tape-recorded interview.
1970b "The Use of Snowmobiles for Trapping on Banks
Island, N.W.T." Paper presented at the Symposium on
Technology and Social Change. American
Anthropological Association Annual Meeting, San
Diego, California.

Index